What Is God Doing?

What Is God Doing?

Lessons from Church History

Lance Lambert

LANCE LAMBERT MINISTRIES

Richmond, VA

Previously Published by
Two-fish Publications
Corona, California

Copyright © 2018
Lance Lambert Ministries
Richmond, VA
USA

ISBN : 978-1-68389-090-4
www.lancelambert.org

Contents

Foreword

The contents of this book, taken from messages spoken at Halford House in Richmond, England, circa 1973–1974, were originally a series of studies on the history of God's people. The final chapter, "The Outpouring of the Holy Spirit," given at a separate time, was added because of its relevance to the subject. The transcripts are lightly edited for clarity and have not been reviewed by the author.

Preface

Throughout the ages, God has been doing one thing which is all to do with His great purpose. As we survey the move of God throughout church history with its apparent ebb and flow, it becomes clear that not even the powers of hell can deter God from preparing the bride and building the eternal city. We today in the twenty first century are a continuation of that forward march and are not a separate entity from the church of previous centuries. Therefore by paying attention to what lies behind us as the people of God, we can be guarded from error and imbalance.

Every successive move of God is like a mini Pentecost with the Spirit of God taking the initiative. Once that happens, it spreads like fire. However, within a generation man interferes by substituting his ideas, ways, and organization for the work of the Holy Spirit and once this departure occurs, the move dies. Nevertheless, what the Spirit of God produces in every move is never lost! Those materials—gold, precious stone and pearl—are deposited into eternity to produce the city of God, the bride of Christ. Therefore, we have every reason to be encouraged, for God Who has taken such care over His people and His work throughout the centuries, will complete what He has begun.

1.
Up to and Including the Reformation

Zechariah 4:1–14

And the angel that talked with me came again, and waked me, as a man that is wakened out of his sleep. And he said unto me, What seest thou? And I said, I have seen, and, behold, a lampstand all of gold, with its bowl upon the top of it, and its seven lamps thereon; there are seven pipes to each of the lamps, which are upon the top thereof; and two olive trees by it, one upon the right side of the bowl, and the other upon the left side thereof. And I answered and spake to the angel that talked with me, saying, What are these, my lord? Then the angel that talked with me answered and said unto me, saying, Knowest thou not what these are? And I said, No, my lord. Then he answered and spake unto me, saying, This is the word of the Lord unto Zerubbabel, saying Not by might, nor by power, but by my Spirit, saith the Lord of hosts. Who art thou, O great mountain? Before Zerubbabel thou shalt become a plain; and he shall bring forth the top stone with shoutings of Grace, grace, unto it. Moreover the word of the Lord came unto me, saying, The hands of Zerubbabel have laid the foundation of this house; his hands shall also finish it; and thou shalt know that the Lord of hosts hath sent me unto you. For who hath despised the day of small things? For these seven shall rejoice, and shall see the plummet in the hand of Zerubbabel; these are the eyes of the Lord, which run to and fro through the whole earth. Then answered I, and said unto him, What are these two olive-trees upon the right side of the lampstand and upon the left side thereof? And I answered the second time, and said unto him, What are these two olive branches, which are beside the two golden spouts, that empty the golden oil out of themselves? And he answered me and said, Knowest thou not what these are? And I said, No, my lord. Then said he, These are the two anointed ones, that stand by the Lord of the whole earth.

Understanding Our History

I would like to devote some time to say a little bit about what lies behind us as the people of God in the twentieth century. I have noticed that the groups, companies or movements which very rapidly go off the rails have always had a very poor regard for all that has gone before them. Their attitude is that everything has failed and now here is something which is absolutely marvelous, self-contained, isolated, able to do everything, and self-sufficient. They believe that God is going to do what He has not been able to do all through the ages. Of course, this is nonsense. This attitude is always held by folks who have no understanding of history, especially the history of the people of God. One of the things that saves us from error and imbalance is a right understanding of what God has been doing through the ages. Indeed, if there was a correct understanding of that little phrase in the Apostle's Creed: "I believe in the communion of saints," it would save us. This does not mean just the fellowship of those who are alive but the unity of all the people of God throughout the ages—those gathered in the presence of God now and those of us still alive on earth.

God Has Been Doing One Thing

We are not a separate entity in the twentieth century, but God has been doing one thing which is all to do with His great purpose concerning the bride of His Son or the city of God, which is another title for the bride, the wife of the Lamb. This amazing spiritual union between Christ and His redeemed people, this formation, as it were, of a people for Himself to be His habitation—which is God's purpose—has never been laid aside. Our Lord Jesus said in Matthew 16:18: "Thou art Peter and upon this rock, [that is Myself, what I am], I-will-build-my-church; and the gates of hell shall not prevail against it."

The Lord Jesus has never stopped building. Even in the darkest era of church history, the darkest part of the age in which we are found, the Lord Jesus has not ceased for one moment to build. He has never laid aside this purpose of the Father, that the eternal city will be produced. This purpose of God has neither been annulled nor brought to nought by Satan, nor has it even been frustrated. Right the way through, the purpose of the Lord Jesus Christ to present to Himself a church without spot or wrinkle or any such thing has never been laid aside. God has not been deterred by men or demons, apostasy, error, false teaching, or any mixture from that which is of Himself. He has not been deterred at all through this age. Not even the combined power and authority of hell has or could deter God from this purpose of His.

Zechariah 4 says this: "The hands of Zerubbabel have laid the foundation of this house; his hands shall also finish it" (see v. 9). We know it was at Pentecost that the hand of the Lord Jesus Christ laid the foundation of the church of God. What is the meaning of Pentecost? It is not gifts nor is it just that we be filled with the Spirit. The meaning of Pentecost is that the Holy Spirit came and entered into a people in order to produce this building of God, and that is exactly what happened. Those 120 units in a congregation suddenly became 120 members of a body. They were no longer merely individual units in a fine and united assembly, but they had a sense of belonging to each other. It is very beautifully put that when Peter stood up to preach, the eleven stood up with him (Acts 2:14). There was an inward sense of belonging. There was no rankling nor was that old spirit of rivalry between them that was always considering who should be first. It had all gone. There was a sense of belonging to one another in all that God was doing.

His hand has laid the foundation of this building, this house, this temple, and His hand is going to complete it. The first three chapters of the book of Revelation are an amazing vision of the church on earth in seven localities and the Lord in the midst of them. These are actually churches on earth—not the church in heaven or in eternity. Before we see anything else such as the great visions, the contortions, the battles, the conflict, the sort of going forward and backward through the chapters from 5 to 19, what do we see? We see the risen glorified Christ in the midst of His churches on earth. He is judging everything and sorting out everything, seeking to bring out what is right and to remove what is wrong. At the end of the book of Revelation all the material which has been produced here on earth is seen in the city of God. The two things are linked together.

God has been working all the way through, including in this age, according to purpose. He has never laid that purpose aside. It is according to that purpose of building or producing the city of God, of producing the bride of Christ that God has continued to work. In Acts 2 we find the prophecy of Joel concerning the Holy Spirit which Peter says was fulfilled on the day of Pentecost, or rather *began* to be fulfilled on the day of Pentecost. It was not completely exhausted on the day of Pentecost because if we look carefully at the prophecy we observe from verses 19–21 that he says:

> *I will show wonders in the heaven above, signs on the earth*
> *beneath; Blood, and fire, and vapor of smoke: the sun shall be*
> *turned into darkness, and the moon into blood, before the day*
> *of the Lord come, that great and notable day: and it shall be,*
> *that whosoever shall call on the name of the Lord shall be saved.*

We know that that great and notable day of the Lord is yet to come and these signs in the sun and moon that we read of in Matthew 24 are yet in the future. Therefore, we understand that this prophecy of Joel concerning the pouring out of the Spirit of

God or the coming of the Spirit of God upon and into us is that we might, in fact, become the stones for the building work of God, so that the Holy Spirit might produce in us the material out of which the city is to be built.

When we look at church history, we find that the Holy Spirit has never abdicated His responsibility. This is one of the most wonderful things about the history of the church. Even in its darkest era the Holy Spirit has never at any single time for one single hour abdicated His responsibility. The Holy Spirit has been given the task of producing the bride and in the last chapter of the Bible we have that wonderful word: "The Spirit and the bride say come" (Revelation 22:17a). Thus, the Holy Spirit has never given up nor abdicated His responsibility; He has never resigned from His position in the work which has been entrusted to Him.

Three Things Found in Every Move of God

We know from church history that every successive move in which God has recovered something has been due to the coming of the Holy Spirit. Wherever we look throughout church history we always find two or three things that have been recovered. One is that the Lord Jesus Christ has become practical Head. The moment He becomes Head in practical terms is when something begins to happen. Secondly, the Holy Spirit is given His rightful place. We cannot know the headship of Christ in practical terms apart from the Holy Spirit's ministry. That is why the Holy Spirit has to be given His place. The third thing which perhaps I should have put first, is that the Word of God is given its rightful place as the sole guide for all matters of life. In every single move of God we will find those three things. There may be many other things that are not so good. There may be other things that are not there or things that are added, but there are these three things in every move of the Spirit of God in this age. Furthermore, the depth and quality of that movement and the time it lasts as a spiritual factor are determined by how long the Lord Jesus, the Holy Spirit, and the Word of God have their place. Whenever any one of those three or all three are contradicted or limited in any way, the departure starts.

The Beginning and the Continuation

Another thing I find very wonderful is in Acts 1:1–2a:

> *The former treatise I made, O Theophilus, concerning*
> *all that Jesus **began** both to do and to teach*
> *until the day in which he was received up.*

Unfortunately, in some of the more colloquial modern versions that little word *began* has been taken out which is a great shame. In fact, it is exactly what the Word says, "began both to do and to teach." The Gospel according to Luke is what Jesus *began* both to do and to teach, and the book of Acts is what the Lord Jesus *continued* to do and to teach. The Gospel according to Luke is the Lord Jesus personally doing and teaching, but in the book of Acts the Lord Jesus is working through His body.

It has always been a great point of debate as to whether the book of Acts was ever finished. There are many New Testament scholars that say quite strongly that there is no proper finish to the book of Acts. Did something untoward happen to Luke so that he never properly finished it? Was it left deliberately open-ended? J. N. Darby as well as Watchman Nee and others believed very strongly that the book of Acts is not finished. In other words, it has continued to be the story of the Lord Jesus doing and teaching through His body throughout the ages. Now this is simply wonderful because it means that one day when we are all finally gathered together in the glory and the former things have passed away and the new things have come in—not only inwardly to our heart but outwardly as well—when there is a new heaven and a new earth, we shall hear the book of Acts from heaven's point of view. We shall hear the whole story related to us of how the Lord Jesus went on doing and teaching right through the successive centuries of this age until the top stone was brought forth.

The Testimony of Jesus

We get a little picture of the lampstand in Zechariah which is really a symbol of the Testimony of Jesus. What is the Testimony of Jesus? It is the people of God holding together something with which we have been entrusted. We have been made one with God in our Lord Jesus Christ. We have eternal life and that is our testimony. The witness is this, that God gave unto us eternal life and this life is in His Son. "He that hath the Son hath the life" (see 1 John 5:11–12). That is the Testimony of Jesus.

It says in Revelation 19:10 that the Testimony of Jesus is the spirit of prophecy. What does that mean? It does not mean only that the testimony of Jesus is that which has inspired the prophet, although that is true. In one sense, all the prophets have been inspired by the Testimony of Jesus, that is, by what they have seen of the goal of God for which our salvation is a means of bringing us into that goal. It is true that all God's grace, all His workings and energies are toward that end, but it means much more. The Testimony of Jesus is the spirit of prophecy which means that when we have the life of God corporately we become prophetic. This is not just an actual prophetic gift but we become prophetic in our nature and character. In other words, the church becomes the means by which all the principalities and powers are instructed. It is the mind of God on any given subject. It is not just teaching but the expression of the mind of God. It can be explanation, an interpretation, a prediction, but always it is the mind of God—and this is what we are.

Wherever you look in church history when God has been doing something and it really has been the Testimony of Jesus, it has been prophetic in nature and content. Those people have become, as it were, the touchstone by which nations have been either made or destroyed. Britain became great because she became a haven for the people of God. God lifted Britain to great heights because she protected and guarded the Word of God. This is also found in other nations where there has been some concern for the rest of the earth, some fear of God, and where there has been some reverence for the Word of God. Where there has been some application of the principles of God's Word to government and national life, God has honored that nation. "Righteousness exalteth a nation; sin is a reproach to any people" (Proverbs 14:34).

Conversely, when there has been the other side such as persecution, that nation has never been honored. This is one of the reasons why there are some nations in Europe who did things to the people of God and they have never recovered from it. I could give example after example but I do not want to upset people. There are plenty of examples in Europe of nations who did the most terrible things to the people of God and have, since then, been poor, backward, and never risen to the heights.

This people of God—not just individual Christians—but the children of God who are being built together and holding the testimony, have become the touchstone of everything. The way they are dealt with has often become the very judgment of that nation. For example, the great Roman Empire and its persecution of the Christians was finally overcome by the gospel it sought to destroy.

After the first outburst of glory and life at Pentecost, during the following twenty to sixty years, there was a great reaction by Satan. To begin with there was an outward reaction of terrible persecution, mass martyrdom, and much else along that line which had begun much earlier. But when the enemy learned by taking that kind of action he got nowhere because more and more people got saved, which made the testimony stronger and stronger, he changed his tactics and began an inward assault. The result of this tactic was that he almost won.

How did he conduct this inward assault? He did it by mass conversion in the third century. Thousands upon thousands of people became Christians because it was popular to become a Christian. The great Emperor Constantine had become a Christian along with his mother, the Dowager Empress. She was the lady who went all around Israel deciding where these shrines should be that some so love. The fact is that by their conversion (we do not know how real their conversion was) overnight it became popular to become a Christian. The Devil had already been working from the inside so that priests and clergy were more concerned about membership, numbers, prestige, and things like this rather than spiritual principles. When this great mass conversion started, they did not bother too much about whether people were really saved. Thus, huge crowds of people came into the church who were only Christian in name.

From that point a political and religious union took place between State and church. The church became a tool of the State and the State became a tool of the church, and this unholy wedding took place which was to produce child after child that was devilish all down through church history. Everything then appeared to be lost. Nevertheless, although there was a marked and progressive decline, the Testimony of Jesus was still held. In all the darkness there were some remarkable movements which were bitterly persecuted. I will give a whole number of names which may appear to be quite unusual and tell a little bit about some of these remarkable movements which from the very beginning appeared in the history of the church. I think you will see that there is a marked similarity between them and what God is doing in our own day and, indeed, what God has done in every single part of church history at the beginnings of all these great movements of the Spirit of God from the Reformation onward.

Until the last century or so we had to rely entirely for information about these groups upon those who martyred them. The most extraordinary thing was that those who opposed and persecuted these groups called all kinds of people one thing. For instance, the term "Nestorian" was used century after century for anybody whom the church felt was not quite on the mark. It was not strictly nor carefully used. Now this is a problem because we only have what the Byzantine or Catholic Church says about these people, but when we read between the lines, we find some remarkable things. Furthermore, where the answers of these people have been preserved we find even more extraordinary things. In the last century or so due to all the archaeological work that is going on all over the world, a good deal more has been discovered and there are some very, very interesting facts beginning to emerge.

We will look at the story of the age in which we live in three periods: The first will be up to the Reformation, then the actual Reformation, and finally the period from the Reformation until now. In this chapter we shall only cover the pre-Reformation period through the Reformation era as a bird's eye view.

The Pre-Reformation Era

Montanists

During the whole of this period there were remarkable movings of the Spirit of God at different points in the centuries right up to the fifteenth century. The first one that I will point out are the *Montanists* who lasted for about four hundred years. They were given the name of a brother by the name of Montanist, who was born in Phrygia, which is central Turkey, in 156 AD. It was only 156 years after the birth of Christ when this movement began, and it was at the point in time when real decline was starting.

They refused to call themselves Montanists; instead they called themselves Christians. They refused any other label or name. They stood for reform within the growing Catholic system. They were seeing the start of the whole system which has developed into the Roman Catholic Church on the one hand and the Orthodox Church on the other.

These dear believers stood against all that they saw beginning to develop and for a complete reform within the whole system, a return to what they called "primitive principles." Now they were just over a century after Pentecost; yet they were already standing for a return to primitive principles—back to what they called primitive piety, godliness, purity and methods. They emphasized particularly the ministry of the Holy Spirit and they said: "The miraculous presence of the Holy Spirit is given to us for the whole of this age." They were therefore charismatic in nature. They spoke in tongues, they had prophecy, and they had all the gifts. This is one of the reasons they caused a tremendous rumpus because most of these had disappeared and already there was the idea that they should die out. So when these godly people began to know the government of the Spirit of God in their midst, leading them into His will, and using whomsoever He would, it naturally caused quite a concern.

They rejected the inclusion in the church of those who were not born again, and they resisted the growing control of the church by bishops. Finally, after trying to stay within the system, they came out in clear separate congregations in the third century. That was of course the time when the state union took place. So they resisted it all the way through until the union took place and they finally came out in separate congregations.

Many have heard of one of the greatest of the church fathers whose name is Tertullian. Tertullian is considered by nearly all to be the most spiritual of the church fathers. However, what is not generally known is that Tertullian severed his link with the Roman Catholic Church and completely threw in his lot with the people who were called Montanists. These are his own written words concerning it:

> *Where but three are and they of the laity [that is the congregation], also yet there is a church.*

Now in days when the movement had become systematized you can understand how remarkable that was. The Montanists lasted for four centuries, and as they began to die much became formalized in the end.

Cathars and Novatians

Then we have another group called Cathars. They are often called *Novatians* or *Puritans*, and they rejected all three of these labels. From the beginning they went outside of the Roman Catholic and Orthodox system and formed companies of believers insisting that they had unbroken succession of testimony from the apostles. They lasted three hundred years from the fourth to the sixth centuries. They were named by others after a man called Novatian who was one of the leaders amongst them. But they themselves refused to call themselves Novatians or Cathars or Puritans

The Catholic Church always was a little afraid of calling people Montanists because of Tertullian. But they called everyone from there, right down to Luther, Cathars. It is one of the dirty words in church history much like *Pentecostals*.

Donatists

Donatists were very much like the Cathars only they were very strong on discipline. They were called Donatists on the North African Coast and, generally speaking, Cathars in Europe. They were also very numerous; indeed they took over nearly everything in the North African churches. They were named after two of their leaders who were both called Donatists, but they themselves refused to label themselves at all except to be known as Christians.

Priscillianists

Then there was another very interesting group called *Priscillianists*. They came from a Roman Catholic priest called *Priscillian* who lived in Spain, and whom God converted. He began to read and study the Word of God and when the Spirit of God came upon him, he began to understand the Word as never before, and he began to teach it. Literally, hundreds of people where he lived got saved and then it began to spread all through Southern France, Portugal and Spain. They were given the name Priscillianists although in actual fact they refused to call themselves anything other than Christians. In the end he was martyred. This was in the fourth century and lasted for two centuries.

They believed that the Word of God was the sole authority for all life and practice. This took place long before the Reformation, but this group of believers went all over Spain, Portugal and the South of France preaching what later was established in the Reformation. They believed in the priesthood of all believers, not only as a doctrine but in practice. In all their simple gatherings, the Holy Spirit could use any one whom He chose. The movement lasted for two centuries right up to the sixth century. It became another very dirty word in church history.

Nestorians

The *Nestorians* were named after a bishop called *Nestorius* who was deposed for so-called heresy. We now know that another gentleman, one of the church fathers called Cyril, was very jealous of Nestorius. This has now come to light and it was basically due to his jealousy that Nestorius was deposed. (We know something of that kind of mudslinging in our own day.) He was deposed and went off to an Egyptian oasis where he spent the rest of his days, but a movement spread all through the East and it was called Nestorian. They gave the name to every single believer or group of believers who would not join in with the Roman Catholic or Orthodox system. They were called Nestorians, but they themselves refused such labels saying that they were the churches of our Lord Jesus Christ. These people were the great missionaries of this period. They carried the gospel right across central Asia to China and into India.

About 130 years ago a great commemorative plaque was found in Central China saying how missionaries had come preaching of a certain Jesus and that many people had been saved in that area along with some bishops. It was hardly credible to most people at the time but it was the first evidence we ever had that the Nestorians went as far as China where they not only preached the gospel but planted the church of God there. This was in the sixth century and their work actually lasted for quite a few centuries both in Central Asia, India, and China. It faded out for one simple reason—they never reduced the Word of God to the spoken language of the people. Therefore, because no one was able to read the Word, superstition gradually took over and it died.

Celtic Christians

Then we come to something more familiar which is *Celtic Christians*. One would not think perhaps that they had much part in this but they have a very big place. All through Britain there were congregations of believers simply meeting together as believers in the fifth and sixth century. Patrick, of whom there is so much trouble these days in Ireland, was born in Scotland near Kilpatrick and was captured by a band of Irish pirates or marauders, and taken to Ireland where he worked on a farm as a herdsman for some years. He had very godly Christian parents but he himself was not interested in their faith. When he was taken away, however, his thoughts returned to his parents and their teaching and he was converted. After six years he gained his freedom and returned to his own people in Scotland.

Upon his return he heard God calling to him in a vision while on the Scottish Coast. He saw a vision, as it were, of the Irish Coast and heard God calling him to come back to Ireland. Patrick returned to Ireland but he had a very hostile time with the pagans who were a type of Viking. Nevertheless, due to his preaching out in the fields where everyone came to hear him, thousands upon thousands were converted. In the end the whole island was evangelized.

About a century later Columba (known to many as *Saint Columba*), who was converted through this movement in Ireland, sailed to Scotland believing that he was called by God to go to Scotland and preach to the Scots. He went to Iona where he discovered a native community already gathered but very weak. There he founded one of the greatest centers for the propagation of the gospel that these islands have ever known. From Iona they sent out missionaries over the whole of Britain, up to central Europe and, of course, to Scandinavia where they brought the gospel.

It was in 563 that the community in Iona was established. Many people have the idea due to later literature from Catholic sources that the Iona community was a monastic community. It was nothing of the kind; it was a community of monks but they were married. They were not required to be married but nevertheless they were, which was slightly different to the Catholic system. Secondly, if you read the actual story of Iona, their whole idea was very much like the kind of life we are familiar with—Bible study, prayer and the sending out of groups of men as missionaries. They went out to different communities where they would build a meeting place surrounded by houses.

They would then bring in the nationals wherever they were, learn the language, teach them, and translate the Scriptures to their tongue as best they could. When they had established a church there of nationals, they would send out twelve—always twelve—to another place and start again. These are what we call the Celtic Christians.

Many have probably heard, as I have, that much of real Christianity began later with Augustine. This is not the famous Augustine of Carthage who wrote the *Confessions*. This was a wicked old man sent by the Pope with forty Benedictine monks with a huge amount of money. He came to Canterbury in Kent and bribed the king of the Angles to get him to go over to Roman Catholicism. He did so and the whole of the Anglo Saxon community followed suit. But the real Britains and the Celts—the Welsh, the Irish, the Scots and the Cornish—refused to accept the Anglo Saxon outlook and there was much trouble as we know from British history. It went on for about two centuries until finally the Celtic Christians lost out and the whole thing came under the sway of Rome. It is an amazing chapter in church history in ancient British Christianity.

Paulicians

Then there is another group called *Paulicians* which we do not know so much about. It is unclear when the movement actually began. If we accept what they themselves say, it began from the beginning. They claimed that they had an unbroken succession through the Cathars right back to the apostles. How they got the name Paulicians is also quite obscure, but it is possibly because of their understanding and emphasis on Paul's letters. Unlike the Roman Church which emphasized Peter very much, they emphasized the teaching of Paul. They were very numerous in Armenia and in Turkey and they did not call themselves Paulicians but Christians or brothers. They claimed to be the true apostolic church of the Lord Jesus Christ. They recognized the independence of each congregation. They taught that spiritual unity is found not in teaching, but in life in Christ. That has a ring that many of us would understand. They repudiated infant baptism. They said that the church ought to pray for children of believers in a special way when they were born. Baptism for those who requested it was by immersion and it was a testimony of repentance and faith in Christ. They also believed that elders should govern each church. We understand now just what a tremendous thing this was. These were people who believed in baptism by immersion for believers only, ones who believed in dedication of children, and elders governing the church. These facts have been obscured for many centuries but they are all there. *Paulicians* was also another dirty word right the way down through church history.

Bogomils

Then there was an extraordinary group that probably came out of the Paulicians. The Paulicians, as I have mentioned, were very numerous in Turkey and Armenia. This group was called *Bogomils*, which was a terrible name. They were found mostly in Bulgaria, Yugoslavia and Macedonia. It is more likely that they traced their beginnings from the Paulicians who were forcibly moved by the emperor to Bulgaria. Bogomils is a very old Slav word meaning "friends of God" or "those dear and acceptable to God."

They flourished from the ninth to the thirteenth century, and the greatest area that was touched was Bosnia in modern Yugoslavia. They so affected Bosnia that even today the prosperity they brought through hard work and consciousness is proverbial. There were thousands upon thousands of them so that the Catholic Church was quite unable to destroy them. I will read something from church history which is just a little description of the Bogomils:

> *There were no priests or rather the priesthood of all believers was acknowledged. The churches were guided by elders who were chosen by lot, several in each church, an overseer called 'Grandfather' and ministering brethren called leaders and elders who moved between the churches. Meetings could be held in any house and the regular meeting places were quite plain—no bells, no altar, only a table on which might be a white cloth and a copy of the gospels. A part of the earnings of the brethren were set aside for the relief of sick believers and of the poor and for the support of those who traveled to preach the gospel among the unconverted.*

Now when you think that that goes right back to the ninth century you understand that here was another remarkable movement of the Spirit of God.

Waldenses & Albigenses

Then we come to another group called *Waldenses* or even more awkwardly *Albigenses*. No one knows where or when these two groups began but possibly it was from the very beginning in the Roman persecution of Nero. The Waldensian Church is very proud of the fact that it is not a separatist movement from the Roman Catholic Church. It never had any union with it and never came out of it so we do not know where or how it began. We do not even know where it got its name. Some people suggest that it was from a brother by the name of Peter Waldo who was a businessman from Lyon. He preached the gospel and became a great leader amongst them but we do not really know.

It is the same with the Albigenses. The Waldenses were the most numerous in the southern valleys of the Alps and the Albigenses were in the south of France. They also were a very great movement of the Spirit of God and especially numerous and influential from the twelfth to the fifteenth century. They had simple gatherings of believers *as believers*. They put no circle around themselves and they had no membership. Anyone could come in so long as they were a believer, even if they were a Catholic. Baptism was upon their testimony of faith in Christ. The Lord's Table was a remembrance of His death and not an actual sacrifice. Elders ruled the church and apostles went among the churches. Due to this particular movement, because it was so widespread and so spiritually virile, the Roman Catholic Church decided to withdraw the Scriptures from the people. They were no longer allowed to read the Scriptures on fear of excommunication.

This was because they were so afraid of what happened amongst these people.

Through all those years the Spirit of God kept alive the Testimony of Jesus in the midst of the darkness which surrounded them. Below is part of a quote from a remarkable document written in 404 which has to do with this portion of church history and is preserved in Strasburg. It is written by an enemy but contains a quotation from one of the brethren. This is the quotation that is so remarkable. It is from a Christian:

For 200 years our fellowship has enjoyed good times and the brethren became so numerous that in their counsels seven hundred or more persons were present. [That is of delegates from churches, not a congregation.] God did great things for the fellowship. Then severe persecution broke over the sons of Christ. They were driven from land to land and to the present time this cruelty continues. But since the church of Christ was founded, the true Christians have never been so far reduced that in the world or at least in some countries some of the saints have not been found.

Also, our brothers, on account of persecution, have at times crossed the sea and in a certain district have found brethren but because they did not understand the language of the country, intercourse with them was difficult and they had to return. The face of the church changes like the faces of the moon. Often the church blossoms on account of a number of the saints and is strong on the earth. Then again she seems to fall and to pass away entirely. But if she disappears in one place, we know that she is to be seen in other lands even if the saints are few who lead a good life and remain in the holy fellowship of Christ. And we believe that the church will be raised up again in greater numbers and strength. The founder of our covenant is Christ and the head of our church is Jesus the Son of God.

That person was martyred for his testimony. But we can see it shows something of the kind of spirit of these people all the way through this downward decline of the church, right down to the fifteenth century. Throughout the centuries there have been groups which were not so huge, in one sense, but who kept alive the Testimony of the Lord Jesus Christ.

The Reformation Era

What can we say about the actual Reformation era? In spite of all these amazing movements about which we wish we knew a good deal more, the darkness which had settled on Christendom was progressive. A huge mountain of difficulty—impossible, insuperable, and immovable—stood between the purpose of God and its fulfillment. Yet God had said His hand laid the foundation, His hand shall also finish it (see Zechariah 4:9). Jesus said: "Upon this rock I will build my church" (see Matthew 16:18). "Not by might, nor by power, but by my spirit" (see Zechariah 4:6). When we come to the fourteenth century all appears as dark and as impossible as could be. Here however we learn one of the greatest and most wonderful lessons of all. It is Christ Himself who said, "I will build my church." Nothing can or will stop Him.

When all seemed darkest, God stepped in and the miracle took place. The actual Reformation is a miracle that very few of us down here will ever understand.

I am going to briefly give five names in connection with the Reformation. I also want to point out many fascinating things concerning different groups of which we are all more familiar. In some ways, these five are the key to the Reformation.

John Wycliffe

First of all is John Wycliffe, who was born in 1320, at the beginning of the fourteenth century. He has been called the "Morning Star of the Reformation." He became an eminent Oxford scholar, fearlessly attacking error and exposing hypocrisy in the church and government. He denied the infallibility of the Pope, the infallibility of the Councils of the church, and transubstantiation. He declared that all, including the Pope and the Councils of the Church, *must* obey the authority of Scripture. Naturally he aroused the fury of the Church. He was brought before the bishops of London with both the Archbishop of Canterbury and the Archbishop of York present on a charge of heresy. They had already decided to burn him at the stake in spite of his tremendous popularity, not only with the common people but also with the nobility of the country, when London had one of its only two earthquakes in recorded history.

The bishops were so afraid that they adjourned the session and never reconvened it. Wycliffe died in peace many years later having nearly destroyed the Catholic Church in Britain.

After this, they forbade him to preach so he gave himself to translation work and writing tracts. They were not the kind of tracts we think of but very weighty on such things as the question and origin of authority, which went to the root of things in the whole country. He translated the Bible from the Latin Vulgate to English.

Lollards

Wycliffe organized bands of preachers who went out two by two over the whole of Britain. These people were called Lollards but do not know why. It could mean that they babbled because this is a very old English word which could mean babbler. In other words, it was a term of derision, or it could mean that in their meetings they seemed to loll around a bit while worshipping the Lord. (I must say we might be called *Lollards* after a Sunday morning meeting.) They went over the whole land preaching the gospel in contemporary style and language. Their influence on the British nation was tremendous. It was said by one of their enemies that two men could not be found together in the whole realm and one of them not be a Lollard. Congregations of believers came into being in many places, especially in East Anglia. They had been saved through the preaching of Lollards and they discovered each other in fellowship. Many of them were burned at the stake. We have a little book in the library which has never been republished called *The Cloud of Witnesses*. It is alphabetical but unfortunately, we have only M to Zed. In that book there is account after account of these Lollards and their last words as they were cruelly murdered. The Lollards suffered in Britain and hundreds upon hundreds of them were burned at the stake for their faith in Christ. Wycliffe died in peace in 1384. The Church could not be outdone by him and almost sixty years later in a special council they condemned him as a heretic, dug up his remains, degraded them and then burned them in 1428. However, it was said of him that "He lit a fire which shall never be put out in the history of England."

John Huss (Jan Hus)

The second man I want to mention is John Huss (Jan Hus), born in 1369. Jeremy of Prague heard Wycliffe in Oxford and caught fire. He returned to Czechoslovakia, then Bohemia, and began to preach the gospel everywhere. John Huss caught fire listening to Jeremy, and the result was a tremendous awakening and revival which spread throughout Bohemia and amongst the Czech-speaking people and throughout Central Europe. People not only got saved but they began to gather together as believers. In one place in Tabor they had huge conventions where they had the Lord's Table with both the cup and the bread. We know that in Roman Catholic practice it is forbidden to give the cup to the people. But they met together in Tabor and down at the bottom of the summit there is still what is called to this day *Jordan* referring to a pool in which they baptized those on profession of their faith. It was a tremendous awakening and revival.

The Council of Constance convened in 1414 and summoned John Huss to come to them to defend his teaching. He decided to go and was given a safe conduct pass by the Emperor in order to preach the gospel before such a gathering of prelates, cardinals, nobles, kings and princes. But when he arrived, he was not given an opportunity to speak but was flung into a dungeon where he was terribly tortured. They tried all the way through to get him to recant, but he would not. He remained in peace to the end and the last letter that he wrote just before he died is perhaps one of the most beautiful documents in church history. Finally, he was taken out, degraded publicly and burned at the stake in 1415. His martyrdom achieved much more than even his life.

United Brethren, "Unitas Fratrum"

Out of all this came the United Brethren, *Unitas Fratrum,* of Bohemia. They were linked to the Lollards in England and to the Waldensians and Albigenses everywhere else with this amazing link. We can see how it is all connected—Wycliffe to Jeremy, Jeremy to Huss and all that happened out of Huss, then back to the Lollards and over to the Waldensians and the Albigenses. The moving of the Spirit of God is most amazing. This was all before the actual Reformation but led up to it. They were to greatly influence Luther at the beginning of the Reformation. It is one of the great questions of church history. Luther was tremendously influenced by the United Brethren. Indeed, he was so influenced by them at one point that he thought they had found the New Testament constitution of the church and was going to introduce it to Germany. Then, unfortunately the Peasants' Revolt began and the excesses of the prophets and what they called *Anabaptists.* Luther thus shot back in fear, being a great conservative, and he reintroduced a more Roman Catholic form of government. It is very interesting that the United Brethren so deeply influenced the course of the Reformation.

Erasmus

The third person I want to mention is Erasmus. Born in 1466 at Rotterdam in Holland, he was educated in one of the schools of the United Brethren in Holland. The United Brethren began a whole series of schools all over Europe wherever they could. Erasmus himself said that he got his love of learning and investigation from the school of the United Brethren. In 1516 he published his *Greek New Testament* with a new Latin translation. This perhaps does not mean much to most of us, but it was like the first atom bomb being set off. Up to then everything had been the *Latin Vulgate*, which was the authorized version of the Church. No one was allowed anything else. Now for the first time someone had gone right back to the fountainhead and had actually taken the text and published it with a new Latin translation! The cheek of it! A new Latin translation, unauthorized by the Church! It was just like a bomb going off in Christendom. This one single event was to influence the course of history more than anything that had been done before. He took people back to the fountainhead. Some people think Erasmus was a compromiser because he never came out of the Roman Catholic Church. Below are some of his notes in the Latin translation. We can understand why these people were burned at the stake although he was not.

Writing of the friars as the traveling monks he says:

Those wretches in the disguise of poverty are
the tyrants of the Christian world.

Speaking of bishops he said:

They destroy the gospel, they make laws at their will,
tyrannize over the congregation and measure right and
wrong with rules constructed by themselves. Who sit,
not in the seat of the gospel, but in the seat of Caiaphas
and Simon the Sorcerer, they are prelates of evil.

Of priests he wrote:

There are priests now in vast numbers, enormous
herds of them, seculars and regulars and it is
notorious that very few of them are chaste.

Of the Pope he said:

I saw with my own eyes Pope Julius II marching at the head of
a triumphant procession as if he were Pompeo Caesar. Saint
Peter subdued the world with faith, not with arms or soldiers
or military engines. Saint Peter's successors would win as
many victories as St. Peter won if they had Peter's spirit.

Of the singing of choristers in the churches he wrote this in his
notes (all of which is published in his *Greek New Testament* Latin
version):

Modern church music is so constructed that the
congregation cannot hear one distinct word. A set of
creatures, who ought to be lamenting their sins, fancy
they can please God by gurgling in their throats.

We can understand why some of these men got into trouble!
It has been said that Erasmus laid the egg which Luther
hatched. He died in his seventieth year without a priest,
which was absolutely remarkable, calling upon the mercy of the
Lord Jesus Christ.

Now here we should just mention three things which God
was using. First He was using the Renaissance which was a
great revival interest in Greek and everything to do with the old
classical world. This is why, because of the Turks invading Europe,
many Greek speaking scholars came into Europe and with
them they brought old ancient Greek manuscripts. This began a
tremendous renewal of literature and interest. That is how we got
our Greek New Testament again. Erasmus was one of the leaders
of what they call the Humanists of his day.

Secondly, in about 1450, the middle of the fifteenth century,
came the invention of printing. This was absolutely of God.
At the same time as the Greek New Testament came, there was
the possibility of translating it into the mother tongues of all the
different nationalities of Europe; thus came printing which gave
a possibility of pouring out thousands upon thousands of books!

Thirdly, of course, came a revival of nationalism. God used all
three things in the Reformation.

William Tyndale

The fourth person I want to mention is William Tyndale born in 1494. It became his lifelong ambition to translate the Bible into good contemporary English. When he was spoken to by a learned theologian, who was sent to convert him from the error of his ways, he said to this bishop, "If God spares my life ere many years, I will take care that a ploughboy shall know more of the Scriptures than you evidently do." He had to flee England for his life. As a lonely exile he went to Germany and worked on his translation of the New Testament conferring with Luther. It was published in 1526 and became the greatest single influence upon the English-speaking world. William Tyndale was martyred near Brussels in 1536. First he was bound by chains to a great crucifix, then he was strangled, after which he was burned. Before he was strangled he cried out in prayer: "Oh Lord, open the eyes of the King of England!" Within two years, in 1538 by royal proclamation, by that wicked man, Henry the VIII, a Bible was placed in every single church in the realm. It had been written in the mother tongue, English, so that it could be read to all people who wished to hear it. William Tyndale's prayer was answered.

Martin Luther and Other Contemporaries

The fifth group of men I want to mention is Martin Luther and other contemporaries. He was born in 1483. With Martin Luther the day of the Reformation was fully come. Luther was just the man the Holy Spirit needed—fearless, robust, full of humor, very much down to earth, contemporary, and with a great gift of putting profound matters simply. By 1517 three matters had become absolutely clear:

1. Man is justified by faith alone in the Lord Jesus Christ.
2. Every believer has direct access to God through Jesus Christ.
3. The Bible is the sole source of authority for faith and life.

These three things may not seem much to us because they are now household matters. We have become so used to this recovery of the Spirit of God that we all take this for granted. But each one of these three things constitutes a tremendous recovery. They undermined a whole system which was satanic:

Man is saved, not by good works, nor by penances, nor by his own righteousnesses, but by faith alone in Jesus Christ.

Every believer has direct access to God through Jesus. You do not need a Pope or priest, confessional or even church, to get to God. That undermined a whole system. We have to understand that the whole authority of the clergy was very largely based on this matter of mediation.

The Bible is the sole source of authority for faith and life— not the church fathers nor the councils of Nicaea nor any other council but the Bible itself. Thus the great foundation stone had been recovered and has never again been lost. We have a flow and an ebb, a going back, but what was gained in recovery was never lost in the subsequent ebb. This is so wonderful and it is all the way through as we shall see.

Luther went just so far. I have a letter in one of Luther's books which I found very interesting because of the new honesty since the last World War. Up to then there has not been a lot of honesty in our various denominations because we have all been self-protective, but now there is a much greater honesty. A Lutheran wrote a remarkable biography of Luther and published for the first time a letter which had been suppressed in which Luther himself said that he wondered about baptism. It was a letter to Philip Melton and he said, "I believe that our brethren in Bohemia may have found the answer and we must keep an open mind on the matter of baptism." Then of course came the terrible excesses of the extremists, and they went back on that.

We must also cover with Luther quite a few others:

Zwingli

Unfortunately, Zwingli died on the battlefield when he was only thirty one years of age. If he had lived to the age that the others lived I think Zwingli would have made a tremendous mark on the church. He had already made it, of course, in Switzerland.

John Calvin

John Calvin was another of the great reformers. These two went farther than Luther. They saw the spiritual nature of the Lord's Table and many other things. They were much clearer on certain things than Luther. There were also many others with these three. Suffice it to say God had done a remarkable thing. He had secured and recovered the foundation stone for the building of the house. Justification by faith, the direct access of every believer to God through Jesus Christ, and the Bible as the sole source of authority for faith and life are really the foundational stones of the whole building.

If I had the time I would have fished out a number of comments by Luther and Zwingli. John Calvin was a little more of a gentleman than Luther or Zwingli. If you have ever ploughed through Luther's commentary on Galatians, you will find he said the most terrible things. I shall never forget when I first studied it. I remember him calling bishops, Catholic prelates, "nitsiks." You can understand the sort of horror that some of these reformers with their down-to-earth type of preaching caused. I remember when I first read the official biography of Ulrich Zwingli and his marvelous comment in the Muenster in Zurich to a packed congregation. He was talking about unction which is the final anointing by oil that is supposed to get you into heaven in Catholic and Orthodox circles. He said, "Better keep the oil for your salad dressing." The reason I bring this up is because people often get the idea that these reformers and others were all rather staid and correct—they were not. One can well understand the fury and the ire that was aroused, not only because what they said was true, but sometimes because of the way they said it! I am afraid that the treasure was in earthen vessels. It always has been and it is something we have to learn right through to the end.

I feel very inadequate when dealing with this but a number of times folk have come to me and said, "I wish you would speak to us about church history." Most people have a horror of history because they have had dopey or drowsy old teachers of history who have given them an everlasting horror of this subject. But in actual fact if we can learn from these things, I think we can be taught tremendous lessons from what God has been doing in the age in which we are found.

Shall we pray?

Lord, we pray that Thou wilt write on our hearts lessons from all this. How we thank Thee for a work of Thy Holy Spirit. How we praise Thee, Lord, for this one thing that Thou hast been doing all the way through church history. We thank Thee for those in every group who have been Thine and we especially thank Thee, Lord, for those groups and those movements in which something has been recovered which has now become for us a household word. Lord, we thank Thee and praise Thee and give thanks also to Thee for helping us in this very hot evening both in speaking and hearing. In the name of our Lord Jesus Christ. Amen.

2.
From the Reformation Onward

Matthew 16:18–19

And I also say unto thee, that thou art Peter, and upon this rock I will build my church; and the gates of Hell shall not prevail against it. I will give unto thee the keys of the kingdom of heaven: and whatsoever thou shalt bind on earth shall be bound in heaven; and whatsoever thou shalt loose on earth shall be loosed in heaven.

Zechariah 4:6–10

Then he answered and spake unto me, saying, This is the word of the Lord unto Zerubbabel saying, Not by might, nor by power, but by my Spirit, saith the Lord of hosts. Who art thou, O great mountain? Before Zerubbabel thou shalt become a plain; and he shall bring forth the top stone with shoutings of Grace, grace, unto it. Moreover the word of the Lord came unto me, saying, The hands of Zerubbabel have laid the foundation of this house; his hands shall also finish it; and thou shalt know that the Lord of hosts hath sent me unto you. For who hath despised the day of small things? For these seven shall rejoice, and shall see the plummet in the hand of Zerubbabel; these are the eyes of the Lord, which run to and fro through the whole earth.

Revelation 10:7

But in the days of the voice of the seventh angel, when he is about to sound, then is finished the mystery of God, according to the good tidings which he declared to his servants the prophets.

I am going to read this next Scripture in William Tyndale's version, the version that was the burden of his heart and for which he died a martyr's death. It is of course the version which underlies our old Authorized Version:

And I saw a new heaven and a new earth: for the first heaven and the first earth were vanished away; and there was no more sea. And I John saw that holy city, New Jerusalem, coming down from God out of heaven prepared as a bride garnished for her husband. And I heard a great voice out of heaven saying, Behold, the tabernacle of God is with men, and he will dwell with them, and they shall be his people, and God himself shall be with them, and be their God. And God shall wipe away all tears from their eyes; and there shall be no more death, neither sorrow, neither crying, neither shall there be any more pain; for the older things are gone. And he that sat upon the seat said, Behold, I make all things new. And he said unto me, Write: for these words are faithful and true. And he said unto me, It is done. I am Alpha and Omega, the beginning and

the end. I will give to him that is athirst of the well of the water
of life freely. He that overcometh shall inherit all things; and
I will be his God, and he shall be my son. Revelation 21:1–7

We have been dealing with the period up to the Reformation with many names of people who continued along that line. Then we dealt with the Reformation era, including Wycliffe, Huss, Jeremy of Prague, Erasmus, Luther, Zwingli, and others. Now I want to go on from this point to all the different recoveries since then.

The Foundation Made Crystal Clear from the Reformation Onward

Finally, after the great battle over the Reformation era, by 1517 three things became crystal clear. First, man is justified by faith alone in Christ and not by his own works. Secondly, every believer has direct access to God through Christ and does not need any priest or clergy to mediate. Third, the Bible is the sole source of authority for all matters to do with faith and life. These three things by 1517 had become crystal clear and this was really the foundation stone—the finished work of the Lord Jesus Christ and the Word of God.

Recovering the Whole Counsel of God

Once the essence or the fundamental principle was in its place, then the Holy Spirit began this great work of recovering the whole counsel of God which had largely been lost and which Luther called "The Babylonian Captivity of the Church." You might think

I thought up that lovely title, but Luther wrote quite an article and preached a number of times on this. He considered the Babylonian Captivity of the Church to be from the church fathers right down to the fifteenth century. He saw it as the church going into exile, becoming a worldly political system, and very much an outward organizational, institutional thing.

In that downward spiral, in spite of these different groups that appeared all the way through and who lived really according to the beginning principles, much of the whole counsel of God was lost. Once this great foundation stone had been recovered the Holy Spirit began to recover the whole counsel of God. I will only mention certain well-defined moves of God.

God's Moves Are Interrelated

In one way or another, the moves of God all overlap and are interrelated. It is easy, in one sense, to speak of them as if they were little independent moves. As we discovered, however, all these groups overlapped and were interrelated, some of them so much so that they were loosely given names. None of the groups took these names but they were given to them by their enemies. These names tended to cover a whole variety of companies and even teachings which had a loose connection together. The same is true in the period of the Reformation. The Albigenses and especially the Waldensians, had much to do with the Reformers. They even sent a delegation to see Farrell in Geneva. They had a great deal of connection with each other; therefore, we cannot speak of each one of them separately. It might be dangerous if we should think of each one being an absolutely independent, indigenous move. They were all related one way or another and drew from others. Just as an example, the Wesley brothers, Charles and John, were both Vicars, ordained ministers of the Church of England. Their great grandfather was one of the men ejected in the Act of Uniformity in 1662 and was an outstanding member. Their great grandfather and grandfather both were Dissenters and Non-conformists. However, their father returned to the established church and John and Charles were born into and brought up in it. Their mother, however, was a Dissenter, and the staunch fire of the great grandfather and grandfather plus their mother's side later came out strongly in the two Wesleys. The point is we cannot say that this was something just completely separate. It all had connections, hence that word of caution.

The Sovereign Intervention of the Holy Spirit

All these successive moves began by a sovereign intervention of the Spirit of God. One of the things that becomes crystal clear as one begins to look at the history of the church is that it was the Holy Spirit breaking in and apprehending a man. Then something happened and through him many others caught fire. Sometimes it was not just one man but a whole group of men. We tend to know one man because by his writings or his influence his name has come down to us but we have forgotten some of the others.

The Puritan Era

The first recovery move was the Puritan Era which was roughly from 1560 until 1670. This name was again loosely given to all who strongly held reformed views. In other words, there were many people that held this view because King Henry and later the other monarchs had adopted the principles of the Reformation which they fell in with. They would have fallen in just as easily with a return to the old ways. Nevertheless, those who were born of God and had the new life in them were called *Puritans*. This was not a name given, as some people imagine, to narrow cranks who hated joy or anything that spoke of a full life; but it was given to a remarkably wide range of people. They were normal, healthy, sound, godly men and women. They were particularly against church vestments, church ornaments, the sign of the cross, the bishops and even organs. There was no problem recognizing them as Puritans because they used to fulminate against these sorts of things at great length. They lived very simply and plainly, believing that any kind of extravagance was really a sign of Romanism and Popery. They flourished especially in the period of the Commonwealth.

It may surprise some to know that for a while Britain was a Republic. For about twenty years of British history, they were called *The Commonwealth*. This was when King Charles I was arraigned before Parliament, sentenced to death and executed. Britain then came under the benign dictatorship of Oliver Cromwell of whom many evil things have been said. Just recently, however, a staunch and devoted Catholic, Lord Langford's daughter, wrote an extraordinary biography of Cromwell which has shown that he was a very warm and broad-hearted man. Under the Cromwellian period, the period of the Commonwealth, in 1642–1660, the Puritans flourished. They came into their own. It was the first time and even afterwards for another one hundred years that the people in Britain had had complete freedom of religion. Regarding all the things said about Cromwell, remember that it was the first time that everyone was allowed to worship God according to their conscience. We owe that to Cromwell.

There is no doubt that the Puritans were a remarkable band of people who really saw something. They were not satisfied with the Reformation. In many ways we could say that John Calvin and John Knox were the fathers of the Puritans. Calvin, who lived from 1509 to 1564 and Knox who lived at about the same time, 1513–1572, both believed, with a number of other men, that the Reformation had not gone far enough and set about inquiring in the Scriptures as to how far the Reformation should go. Of course, Knox was virtually the disciple of Calvin. The result of their endeavor is what we now know as the Reformed Church or the Presbyterian Church of Holland, Switzerland, France (the Huguenot Church) and Scotland, or the Presbyterian Church of Wales which was slightly different because it was the later product of George Whitfield. They were greatly influenced by these two men.

When we read some of the books that these men wrote, we begin to realize just what godly men they were. Far from being dull, dry old dead bones, there is wealth in them. Below are some of their quotes:

An ark for all God's Noahs in a gloomy, stormy day.

Or:

The best wine reserved 'til last.

Or:

The transcendent excellency of a believer's portion
above all earthly portions whatsoever.

This was by Thomas Brooks, a man still in the Church of which there was only one at that time. Notice that he did not call it "Saint Margaret's," he called it "Margaret's New Fish Street." He does not refer to himself as "Vicar" or even "Minister" but "a preacher of the gospel and still a preacher of the Word in London and pastor of a congregation there."

Below is another title from a different man. Note that I am quoting all these from first editions:

Sips of Sweetness or Consolation for Weak Believers - John
Durant, preacher of the gospel in the city of Canterbury.

It does not say whether he was in the cathedral. He says he is just a "preacher of the gospel in the city of Canterbury." Then again, here is another one:

Two treatises, the one handling the doctrine of Christ's
mediatorship wherein the great gospel mystery of
reconciliation betwixt God and man is open, vindicated
and applied; the other of mystical implantation wherein
the Christian's union and communion with the conformity
to Jesus Christ, both in His death and resurrection is
opened and applied. - By John Brinsley, minister of
the gospel and preacher to that incorporation.

Now "to that incorporation" is the church of God at Great Yarmouth and he uses the word "incorporation" meaning those who are incorporated into Christ. "To that incorporation"— is that not beautiful? Now we get some idea as to what these men believed. Do not forget they were all ministers of the Church of England. There were no Non-conformists at that time

Here is another:

The Salvation of the Saints by the Appearances of Christ Now in Heaven, Hereafter From Heaven:

A treatise wherein the appearance of Christ now within the veil in order to the insuring of the salvation of believers and likewise His appearing again a second time to instate believers in that salvation is humbly inquired into and held forth. - By John Durant, preacher of the gospel in Christ's church, Canterbury.

Thus we know it is Christ's Church Canterbury. He does not say *Christ* Church; he says *Christ's* church, Canterbury. So we see how they changed some of the old names.

Here is another. Note that some of these men were later martyred and this is one of them:

An Exposition with Practical Observations Continue upon the Book of Job, - By Joseph Carroll, preacher of the word, pastor of the congregation there.

There are six or seven volumes of this and two or three are bound together in each.

Four Main Groups Within Puritanism

From this we get some idea of these Puritans. Far from being narrow minded, joyless, fusty, dry dead old bones that some people would have us believe, we get an amazing picture of them from their own words. Just by listening to them we begin to see these people are like ourselves. They had seen something and they were seeking to return to something. There were four main groups within Puritanism. At the beginning all of them held together but the tragedy was the division that came. This is the same point in nearly all these moves, that is, the division that came very quickly.

These four groups or lines were not clearly defined until after the restoration of the Monarchy in 1660 and the Act of Uniformity in 1662, whereby all ministers in the Church had to sign a declaration that they would be faithful to the bishops, that they recognized the Sovereign as actual head of the Church on earth, that they would uphold the various sacraments, and so on. This caused absolute consternation in the country and two thousand ministers refused to sign. Now remember there was a small population in those days, perhaps about one million in Britain, and two thousand ministers through conscience, refused to sign the declaration and were ejected from their livings. They were put out on the street. That is how Nonconformity began in Britain. The very best men in the Church were thrown out.

Evangelical Churchmen

Now when they were thrown out they immediately fell, unfortunately, into four groups. There were, of course, the evangelical churchmen who were not thrown out. In some way they managed to twist their consciences and sign the declaration. They were satisfied with the condition of the Church as it was then and they signed the declaration and stayed.

The Presbyterians

The second group, and by far the largest, was the Presbyterians. At first it seemed that the Church of England would become Presbyterian. Indeed, Charles I actually signed a document saying that he believed that the whole Church of England should be formed according to what we now call *Presbyterianism*, and he gave the right to it. However, during the restoration of the Monarchy, Charles II withdrew the document and a great deal of trouble followed. They believed in a Presbyterian form of the Church government which was still wedded to the state. That is very important to note. They stood for elders, which in those days was absolutely revolutionary, instead of the government of the church by bishops. One bishop would have a large area which he governed; but they said the Bible did not teach that! They maintained that every church should be governed by elders and that the elders were bishops with at least two in every church. This is the Presbyterian view and was both Calvin and Knox's view. They also refused to accept that a monarch, who may be debauched, even immoral and unbelieving, should be looked upon as the head of the church on earth. They said they could never accept such a thing. "Jesus Christ," they said, "is the Head of the church on earth as well as Head of the church in heaven." They also believed in synods, which is a coming together of the churches by the sending of delegates from all the different churches. Matters were discussed and decisions were taken which were binding upon the whole. In other words, they believed as we do, that just as individual believers should have fellowship one with another, so the churches should also have fellowship one with another. We should not be alone.

The Huguenots

There are two groups we should mention in particular because they had very great influence upon the Presbyterian Puritans. The first were the Huguenots. They had a tremendous influence through Calvin upon Scotland and indeed upon the whole of Europe wherever Calvinism came in. For instance, they left an influence upon the Netherlands which has never been effaced. The Huguenots, of course, suffered terribly and thousands upon thousands of them fled to Holland, to the Protestant states of Germany, and to Britain and Scandinavia. They brought with them all kinds of crafts and arts which they proceeded to set up in Britain, and thus the Protestant countries became by far the wealthier because of it whereas France became infinitely the poorer. The Huguenots had a tremendous influence because their faith had to go deep within them in order to lose everything for the Lord.

The Scottish Covenanters

The second group was the Scottish Covenanters. They have left an imprint upon Scotland that will never be effaced until the Lord returns. Of course, it all began with the king trying to introduce the Prayer Book into Scotland. Now the Scots have always had an aversion to the Prayer Book which goes right back to the Celtic

Christians. The influence of the Celtic Christians was never really lost in Scotland. When the king tried by law to introduce the Prayer Book in Scotland, it caused a tremendous upset. The result was that because people were rejected and not allowed to have a say in anything nor allowed to be members of the Scottish Parliament, they began to meet out in the Moors. Thus the whole story of the Covenanters began which was just the same as the Huguenot story. There was bitter persecution and wickedness perpetrated by the English upon the Scots which has never been forgotten in Scotland. It has been the cause of very much bitterness down through the years. Interestingly enough, it was William of Orange landing at Torbay that ended the persecution in Scotland. That is why the Ulster people and the Scots are so fond of William of Orange.

Both of these groups, the Huguenots and the Scottish Covenanters, have left an indelible mark upon us.

The Congregationalists or Independents

The next group of the Puritans was the Congregationalists or Independents. This is quite a large group, though not nearly as large as the Presbyterian group. They are sometimes called Brownists after one of their outstanding leaders, Robert Brown. They believed in the independence of each congregational local church. So great was this movement of the Spirit of God that everyone began to investigate the Word of God. "What does the Word of God teach? What is the church? How should we be governed?" It was tremendous. They were not enemies; they were just seeking. Some felt that there should be a federation of churches under synods and Presbyterianism.

Others felt: "No, each congregation is independent. No local church has the right to govern another local church. Every church is equal." They believed in elders, not bishops, as did the Presbyterians. They made a real attempt to bring the people of God together as believers. They refused to divide on the matter of baptism. What they did was this: They said, "We will accept those who believe they should be baptized as believers and we will only baptize the children of whom at least one parent is a born-again believer." Thus it was a kind of compromised arrangement; it was an attempt to bring together all believers as believers.

John Owen

Some of our most famous names in British church history belong to the Independents. Many will have heard of John Owen. He wrote a book which caused such a furor in his day called:

AN INQUIRY into the Original Nature, Institution,
Power, Order and Communion of Evangelical churches.

The first part:

With an answer to the discourse of the unreasonableness
of separation written by Dr. Edward Stillingfleet,
Dean of Paul's [not St. Paul's]; and in defense of
the vindication of Non-conformist from the guilt
of schism. - John Owen, Doctor of Divinity

John Owen, of course, wrote treatise after treatise. He was a tremendous pamphleteer as well as a great teacher. He left his mark upon Congregationalism and upon the Baptists as well.

Isaac Watts

Then there was Isaac Watts. Many know this brother because of the hymns we often sing. He came out of one of these groups of Independents a little later on.

John Robinson

There was also John Robinson who was exiled to Holland. He was not allowed to go with the early fathers to the United States where they felt they would have freedom of conscience to worship God as was right. Below is a portion of his parting message:

I charge you before God and His blessed angels that you follow me no further than you have seen me follow the Lord Jesus Christ. If God reveals anything to you by any other instrument of His, be as ready to receive it as you were to receive any truth by my ministry. For I am verily persuaded that the Lord hath more truth yet to break forth out of His Holy Word. For my part, I cannot sufficiently bewail the condition of those reformed churches which have come to a period in religion and will go at present no further than the instruments of their reformation. The Lutherans cannot be drawn to go beyond what Luther saw. Whatever part of His will our God has revealed to Calvin, the Lutherans would rather die than embrace it. And the Calvinists, you see, stick fast where they were left by that great man of God who yet saw not all things.

This is a misery much to be lamented. For though they were burning and shining lights in their times, yet they penetrated not into the whole counsel of God. But were they now living would be as willing to embrace further light as that which they first received. For it is not possible the Christian world should come so lately out of such thick anti-Christian darkness and that perfection of knowledge should break forth at once.

Now considering that was in 1612, it yet has a modern ring and seems like someone today speaking in those terms.

Baptists

Then there was a fourth group of the Puritans that were called Baptists. They maintained that only believers should be baptized. Now this was not a newfangled notion as was so often said then and since. Paulicians as well as the Bogomils, Waldenses and the Albigenses had all practiced baptism by immersion for believers.

Anabaptists

Following that were the Anabaptists about whom there was so much controversy. The first congregation of Anabaptists met together in Zurich as early as 1525. They were terribly persecuted. No group was persecuted worse than the Anabaptists. This was partly because under the name of Anabaptist came a whole lot of revolutionaries and anarchists. They called anyone Anabaptist who might be a political revolutionary or anarchist, as well as those who were unbalanced, excessive or extreme. The favorite form of execution was drowning. Children, women, as well as men were sown up in sacks and thrown into the rivers of Europe in their thousands. In Salzburg for instance, those many and very beautiful fountains are marred for me forever by the thought and memory that thousands of Anabaptists were drowned publicly in them.

There were sad excesses amongst the Anabaptists of which I will give one example. Jan Matthys and John of Leiden called "The Münster Prophets," both from Holland, believed that they had a command from God to set up the New Jerusalem in Münster, Germany. Earlier a man called Hoffman had believed that he had received in a vision a revelation from God that he should set up the New Jerusalem in Strasburg. Unfortunately, he drove all the Anabaptists out of Strasburg so that was the end of that. I think I am right in saying he was detained in prison where he later died. But these other two took up the fallen standard and went to Münster where, due to the Burgermeisters of the city, they allowed entrance to Anabaptists. Thus Anabaptists poured in from all the persecuted territories so that there were thousands upon thousands of them in Münster. Then began a reign of terror led by these two men who said that polygamy was to be practiced and that marriage was an earthly institution. They had visions, prophesyings, and all kinds of things. This, of course, is what turned Luther away. He became horrified by the whole thing. Finally the Catholics surrounded Münster and there was a most terrible massacre. It was something that was to leave its scar upon the Christian testimony for many years, and the word Anabaptists became a dirty word. It was a terrible thing for anyone to be called an Anabaptist.

Menno Simons and Mennonites

Menno Simons, born a Catholic in Holland in 1496, was another very fine man who redeemed the whole situation. In 1536, having become convinced that infant baptism was wrong, he sought a believer's baptism. He had witnessed the Anabaptists being drowned, including his own brother. Seeking baptism, yet finding no one to do this, he baptized himself and congregations began to spring up in Holland and spread throughout Central Europe and into Russia. They are now known as Mennonites but they themselves never accepted the name Mennonite although they do today.

British Puritans and John Smith

When we come to Britain and the British puritans, John Smith was the first British puritan to become convinced on the matter of baptism. He and others of like mind had to flee England for Holland. In Holland, becoming absolutely convinced of baptism and being unable to find someone to baptize him, he also baptized himself and then baptized the rest of the congregation. Thus in 1609 the first English speaking Baptist church began meeting in Holland. They refused to call themselves a Baptist church; they said they were a gathering of believers or disciples. They stood for the independence of each congregation and for elders. They were against the union of state and church and were democratic in structure, much more so than the Independents. They believed that everyone had a right to say what they felt in the government of the church. Although today we take this for granted, in those days it was *revolutionary*. This is why the word Anabaptist and Communism, in a sense, got mixed up. They felt that these people were wild revolutionaries who would overthrow all government because they believed "one person, one vote." Never forget that it was the Baptists who finally gave us democracy as we know it, that is, one person, one vote.

John Bunyan

I will quote something from Bunyan. Many have heard of John Bunyan's *Pilgrim's Progress*. He was, of course, the most famous of the Baptists and this is his statement:

> *I will not let water baptism be the rule, the door, the bolt, the bar, the wall of division between the righteous and the righteous. The Lord deliver me from superstitious and idolatrous thoughts about any of the ordinances of the Christ and of God. Since you would know by what name I would be distinguished from others, I tell you. I would be and hope I am a Christian and choose, if God should count me worthy to be called a Christian, a believer, or other such name which is approved by the Holy Ghost.*

The early Baptists did not believe that only those who were baptized by immersion should fellowship together. They believed all could fellowship together but they would practice no other form of baptism other than believer's baptism.

Those are the four groups unto which the Puritans flow. They left a mark upon things in the church which has never been eradicated. Every single believer, especially the English-speaking believers owe a tremendous amount to these people. Also note that many of them were martyred; it was a baptism of fire.

The Quakers

George Fox

The next recovery move is the Quakers. I have dated it about 1646 which is the middle of the seventeenth century. The Quakers were one of the most remarkable moves of the Holy Spirit in church history. George Fox was born in 1624. In 1643 at the age of nineteen he left home and started wandering as a kind of hippie up and down the country through hills and fields searching for God. He called this his "agonizing search for God." In 1646, after three years of wandering and inquiring of all kinds of people, talking with both churchmen and dissenters, as he called them, and finding no answer, he was converted through an inward revelation of the Spirit of God. He heard the Lord speak in his heart that he should not search any further but cast himself upon the mercy of the Lord.

The Reformation had become largely an outward matter. There was much legalism and formality, *endless* discussion and bitterness about church government, church forms, church methods, and church rights. John Melton wrote: "The new Presbyter is but the old priest writ large."All over the country were people called "the Seekers." This was a name given to a whole section of people not bound by any denomination or personalities, people who were fed up and sick to death of all the deadness of the Reformation and were seeking for a real inward experience of Christ. They were dubbed "the Seekers" and Oliver Cromwell said of them, "To be a seeker is to be the best sect next to a finder."

George Fox, anointed with the Spirit of God, became a prophet to those seeking souls. Everywhere thousands upon thousands were converted. They became known in the very beginning as "children of the light" because of the great accent of George Fox's preaching on the light of God. Later they became known as Quakers, but we do not quite know why. Some said it was because they sat in silence in their meetings until the Spirit of God came upon them and they shook, especially those who stood up to take part. They were thus called Quakers but this was in derision. Others say it was because when one of them was being judged, he turned to the judge and said, "Judge, you should quake before the Lord of all the earth." To this the judge replied, "I am no quaker." Therefore some say that is how the name came into being but we do not honestly know.

It was only in 1800 that they were called the "Society of Friends." They were against a paid ministry. One of the things that was like a red rag to a bull as far as George Fox was concerned was salaried ministers. There was the famous occasion where in one place the priest was speaking from Isaiah 55:1. The text was: "Ho, every one that thirsteth, come ye to the waters, and buy without money and without price." When Fox could bear it no longer he stood up and said:

You hypocrite! How can you say that it is without price and money when you take 300 pounds a year off this congregation?!

Seeing Everything in Terms of Spiritual Life

Now we can well understand how the early Quakers were disliked. They were very much against the paid ministry in the church and very opposed to outward ordinances. They were also very much against church buildings and refused to call them the church; rather they always called them the "steeple house." They were also very opposed to special dress. They saw everything in terms of spiritual life.

There were some people who said they did not put any emphasis on regeneration; however, this is incorrect. They put a tremendous emphasis upon regeneration as the first step. It is the later Quakers who became wishy-washy and focused more on inner light and revelation. The early Quakers again and again made the point of regeneration. In fact, the way Fox began was by an understanding that the places that were called churches and chapels were not really the church at all but rather the church was the gathering together of truly born again believers, regenerate through the Holy Spirit.

They saw everything in terms of spiritual life. They believed in the priesthood of all believers and the sovereignty of the Spirit of God in all gatherings of believers. This meant the Holy Spirit could lead whomever He wanted to as He chose. They also believed in spiritual gifts. Here is a paragraph from Edward Barrow written in 1652:

> In all things we found the light which we were enlightened
> withal, to be alone and only sufficient to bring to life an
> eternal salvation. And so we ceased from the teachings of

all men and their words and their worship and their temples
and their baptisms and their churches. And we met together
often and waited upon the Lord in pure silence from our
own words and from all men's words and hearkened to the
voice of the Lord and felt His word in our hearts to burn
up and beat down all that was contrary to God in us. And
while waiting upon the Lord in silence, so often we did for
many hours together, we received often the pouring down of
the Spirit upon us and our hearts were made glad and our
tongues loosed and our mouths opened and we spake with new
tongues as the Lord gave us utterance and as the Spirit led
us which was poured down upon us, on sons and daughters.
And the glory of the Father was revealed. And then began we
to sing praises to the Lord God Almighty and to the Lamb.

That has something of a modern ring about it. It is quite remarkable. In 1654 they organized a mission to the whole of England. Sixty or seventy of them went out by twos or threes, mostly young men, speaking anywhere and everywhere, in barns, in the open air and anywhere that they could find. Thousands were converted.

After the restoration they suffered terrible persecution. Indeed, one of their historians writing at the time said, "There was seldom less than 1,000 of us in prison at any one time." I will just quote another portion of the Quakers before we leave them. This is the statement of a man who had just been judged and thrown into prison where he later died. It is his hand-written account:

From the beginning unto this day, and you have gotten
their words to train and paint yourselves with as the Jews

did the true prophets' words, and made a fair outward
profession with garnishing the sepulchers of the righteous
as you do now with crying up the ordinances of Christ
and the ministers of Christ and says, if you had been
in the days of your forefathers you would have not
slain the martyrs that died in Queen Mary's reign.

But we say unto you they suffered by the same murdering
spirit which you manifest to be in you. Who persecute by her
laws and do imprison and falsely accuse under the name of
wondrous seducers and disturbers of your peace the faithful
servants of the Lord Jesus Christ whom He hath called forth of
the words 'made conformable to Him and His death through the
sufferings and renewing of the Spirit in the regeneration.' And
this we declare to you all that do act the things aforementioned
and yet make a profession of faith in Christ, that they who
did in times past, who do now believe in Christ Jesus and
are regenerate and born again through faith in him, are
no persecutors. Neither did they, nor do we who believe in
Christ, persecute falsely, accuse or imprison any that speak
in the name of the Lord and exhort people to repentance.

And we do again declare in the presence of the Lord God
of heaven and earth—and it shall be answered with the
light in all consciences—that you that do imprison, falsely
accuse, persecute and scorn those that declare against
sin in your streets and in your steeple houses under the
names aforementioned, are shut out from amongst all the
saints and children of God that believe in the Lord Jesus.

And you are found in Cain's way who slew his brother.

In the end, these were his last words before being judged:

*And oh dear brethren, companions in the kingdom and
patience of the Lord Jesus who are his faithful witnesses, lift
up your heads and rejoice in the Lord who has counted you
worthy to suffer for His name's sake and stand immoveable
in the life and power of God and be bold and of good courage.
Be of a sound mind and be obedient to the Lord Jesus Christ
and forget the things that are behind and press forward in
the pure light through the straight gate in the daily cross to
that which is contrary to the light. And tread and trample
upon that which would shake your confidences and be
faithful to the end that you may receive a full reward with
all the faithful ones who suffered before you from the Lord
God of Sabbath who is a consuming fire to his enemies but
is, ever was, and abides forever, the refuge of all that trust in
Him. Glory and praise be given to Him forever and ever.*

You would not think this was stated in a courthouse. This is what
it says at the end:

*From the righteous seed whom the world in scorn
calls Quakers, whose bodies are in outward bands
in the common jail in North Hampton.*

There they died. There is no doubt that the Quakers were
to change the face of Britain. They taught us above all else,

the essentially inward and organic nature of the church. They taught us to be very careful about being too dogmatic regarding steps to experience. These people never sang a hymn in the way we know it; however, they rejoiced in the Lord. They did not believe in any kind of music or any kind of emotion. They sat in absolute silence and yet before long the Spirit of God fell upon them and they prophesied and had revelations, visions and moved together under the anointing of God. It is most extraordinary, it is salutary. It stops us from getting too tied up and too dogmatic. These dear people have taught us something. There are people who tell us, even today, that something should and must happen to a person while he is being baptized, yet these people did not even have baptism. They did not have the Lord's Table. They refused to have any type of church pattern, yet inwardly they had it all. They knew more about the meaning of baptism than thousands of people who have been baptized as believers. They lived in the spirit of it. They knew more about communion with Christ and receiving Christ in their hearts than those who take the bread and the wine Sunday after Sunday. Is that not a salutary lesson to us? It teaches us of another great thing that God was recovering. First He recovered the matter of justification by faith and the Word of God. Then it was to do with the independence of congregations and elders and the fellowship of churches and baptism, and later it was to do with the *organic life,* the inward life, the essentially inward life of everything to do with the Spirit.

Methodists and the Great Evangelical Awakening

Now we come to the Methodists in approximately 1740. There could have been few periods in history, certainly for Britain, which were so dark as the beginning of the eighteenth century. Both the State and free church were in a lifeless condition. Quakerism had itself become formal. They started wearing the hats and buckles and using "thee's and thou's" and all the rest of it. Wickedness, lawlessness, and immorality were everywhere. In many places it was not even safe to travel. There were parts of the country one did not dare enter. One such place was Cornwall. No one in his right mind went into Cornwall in the old days. People were terrified of them. It is true that there were house groups meeting together for fellowship and prayer scattered throughout the country, but they were very few and far between.

A little group of students met together in Oxford and amongst them were John and Charles Wesley, and George Whitfield. Although none of them were born again, they used to rise early in the morning for devotions. In 1738 John was converted in a little house group meeting of the Moravian brethren on Fleet Street when Peter Burma read the preface to Luther's Galatians. Again we see the connections, all of them were related—the Moravians, Luther and then we have John Wesley converted. Charles was converted three days before John. We do not quite know when George Whitefield was converted, but it was sometime between 1736 and 1738. Thus began the Great Evangelical Awakening.

Emphasizing New Birth and Holiness

One of the great emphases in this awakening was new birth, whereas before it had been justification. The Wesleys, and Whitfield particularly, preached new birth as an absolute necessity. More than preaching new birth they also greatly emphasized holiness, which was especially stressed by the Wesleys. They said that holiness was a second work of grace, that it was a definite distinct experience that Christians should seek after. It was included in their salvation but they must also seek after it. Now one of the great emphases all the way through Wesleyanism was "going on and possessing." This is heard in their hymns again and again:

Savior from sin, I wait to prove that Jesus is thy healing name.

Note that this is not the song of an unsaved person but of a believer.

Jesus thine all victorious love, Shed in
my heart, my soul abroad.

O thou who camest from above, the pure celestial fire to impart,
Kindle a sacred flame of love on the mean altar of my heart.

There was not a looking backwards to everything and declaring: "I've got it all, I've got it all!" The great emphasis of the Wesleyan and Whitfield so-called Methodist revival was that it was not only a matter of new birth but seeking!—going on, pressing on, entering in. They taught that after salvation you must go on to full assurance and then from full assurance you must move on to perfect love.

When you read some of the hymns of Wesley, you begin to understand. They are tremendous. Unfortunately most of the Wesleyan hymns we now sing have been emasculated. Many of the verses have been cut out because some of them had sixteen to seventeen verses and it became difficult to sing them all, but in those good old days they sang the lot. Furthermore, a good two-thirds of the congregation could neither read nor write, so they had someone teaching them line by line in order to get the truth into them.

One of the great accents in the early Methodist movement, like the Quaker movement, was the "class meeting." These meetings were groups of people meeting together all over the country simply as believers. Some had not yet found the Lord but all could take part as led by the Spirit of God. One would read a portion of the Word, another would give another little word of testimony, and another would suggest a hymn. Someone else might pray or praise the Lord. Wesley said, "When the class meeting dies, Methodism will die." The class meeting did die about the beginning of this century and with it, virtually, Methodism.

Believing Only in One People of God

Below are two hymns which show how these people, like the Quakers (who refused to call themselves Quakers), thought of themselves. They were just children of God, disciples, believers.

It was only later that they accepted the name Quaker. They always referred to themselves as "those called by others Quakers." The Methodists always called themselves, "those called Methodists in scorn by others." In one of Wesley's hymns his preface says: "For people called Methodists by others." They refused to call themselves Methodists in the beginning. Consider the select verses of the following hymn:

Christ from whom all blessings flow,
Perfecting the saints below,
Hear us, who Thy nature share,
Who Thy mystic body are.

Join us, in one spirit join,
Let us still receive of Thine;
Still for more on Thee we call,
Thou who fillest all in all.

Closer knit to thee, our Head
Nourish us, O Christ, and feed
Let us daily growth receive
More and more in Jesus live.

Jesus, we Thy members are,
Cherish us with kindest care.
Of Thy flesh and of Thy bone,
Love, forever love Thine own.

Move and actuate and guide,

Diverse gifts to each divide.
Placed according to Thy will,
Let us all our work fulfill.

Never from our office move,
Needful to the others prove,
Use the grace on each bestowed,
Tempered by the ark of God.

Sweetly now we all agree,
Touched with softest sympathy;
Kindly for each other care;
Every member feels its share.

Wounded by the grief of one,
All the suffering members groan.
Honored if one member is,
All partake the common bliss.

Many are we now, and one
We who Jesus have put on;
There is neither bond nor free,
Male nor female, Lord, in Thee

Love, like death, hath all destroyed,
Rendered all distinctions void;
Names and sects and parties fall;
Thou, O Christ, art all in all!

Here we see what they believed. Far from being a distinct denomination as Wesley said in all his journals:

I am journeying to the people of God in... [so and so].

Or:

I've heard news of the people of God in
... [such and such a place].

He never referred to them as Methodists, or a party, or a sect. Even more marvelous is this hymn which might now be considered unsingable:

Happy the souls that first believed
To Jesus and each other cleaved,
Joined by the unction from above
In mystic fellowship of love.

Meek, simple followers of the Lamb,
They lived, and spake, and thought the same;
Break the commemorated bread,
And drank the Spirit of their Head.

On God they cast their every care,
Wrestling with God in mighty prayer.
They claimed the grace through Jesus given,
By prayer they shut and opened heaven.

To Jesus they perform their vows,
A little church in every house.
They joyfully conspired to raise
Their ceaseless sacrifice of praise.

Propriety was there unknown,
None called what he possessed his own.
Where all the common blessings share,
No selfish happiness was there.

With grace abundantly endued,
A pure, believing multitude,
They all were of one heart and soul,
And only love inspired the whole.

O what an age of golden days!
O what a choice, peculiar race!
Washed in the Lamb's all cleansing blood,
Anointed kings and priests to God!

Ye different sects, who all declare,
"Lo! Here is Christ!" or "Christ is there!"
Your stronger proofs divinely give,
And show me where the Christians live.

Join every soul that looks to Thee,
In bonds of perfect charity;
Now, Lord, the glorious fullness give,
And all in all forever live!

There are many more hymns by Wesley that could be read. I am not being unkind, but we can see what has happened to Methodism. Many of these hymns are not even found in hymn books today. It is tragic. The point is this: All these men in their beginnings believed only in one people of God. They did not believe in some sectarian type of foundation for fellowship.

The Methodists were raised up by a great move of the Spirit, and it changed the face of Britain. The effects of it are still with us today.

The Brethren

I will move on to the Brethren. In 1830, the early part of the nineteenth century, quite spontaneously in a number of centers all over the British Isles, companies of believers came into being in Dublin, Plymouth, Bath, Barnstable, and North Scotland. All over groups sprang up quite simultaneously without any connection with one another. They came together simply as believers. Another extraordinary thing was that they were all breaking bread together. The foundation of their fellowship and gathering was Christ alone. They had no membership and refused to have one. They would have no membership roll, they would have no right hand of fellowship, and in those early days they had no letters of commendation. They accepted people as believers once they were clear that they were believers and that was the ground of their fellowship. They believed that there should be no names, no titles, and no labels at all associated with the church. They believed in the priesthood of all believers *in practice*. That is, under the government of the Holy Spirit, He could use anyone as He wished. In their early days they believed in a definite experience of the Holy Spirit, but unfortunately, as time went on that was quenched along with other matters, and more and more they spoke of that as something that was past, especially the gifts.

It was a tremendous move of the Spirit with worldwide consequences. Of all these different moves, I suppose the Brethren, as far as the recovery of the church, was one of the greatest moves in church history. There were no great flaming personalities in one sense and yet there are hosts of names, many of them household words in Christian circles that are connected with this move—George Mueller, Henry Craik, Robert Cleaver Chapman, Benjamin Newton, J. N. Darby, J. G. Bennett, C. H. Macintosh, C. A. Coates, Anthony Norris Groves, and George Wigram. They were not just untaught, unlettered people either. Many of our best Hebrew commentaries, Bible lexicons, dictionaries, and even our Greek New Testament dictionaries were produced by the Brethren. It was a tremendous move.

One of the great things they emphasized was the coming of the Lord. This was one of the greatest recoveries at that time. Of course, believers always believed that the Lord was coming again, but the Brethren defined it very, very clearly; actually almost too much. That was another very great move.

Pentecostalism and Related Moves

Then we come to another move in 1906 which was Pentecostalism. There were a number of preparatory movements that led up to it. A.B. Simpson, in many ways, must be thought of as the father of Pentecostalism. He exercised a tremendous ministry in the United States and the effects of his ministry spread pretty well worldwide. He taught unrelentingly that he believed in healing for the body, in a definite experience of holiness, and in an anointing of the Holy Spirit. These three things, as it were, began to permeate into Christian circles.

The Irvingite Movement

Much earlier than the Pentecostal movement, as early as 1832 and almost contemporary with the Brethren, was the Irvingite Movement. Edward Irving was an extraordinary man. He was an actor who was converted and then became an outstanding preacher. He began to see what God was seeking after and began to talk very much about recovery. Then, unfortunately, the movement became caught up in other things. They believed in twelve apostles and that the church could only meet when an apostle was present. That is why when visiting some places in London, Edinburgh and Glasgow one can see great big magnificent church buildings which are no longer used because the apostles have long since died. No one thought to replace them with others and thus they are not allowed to meet. It is a terrible state of affairs. Yet the Irvingites were extraordinary. In the middle of the last century they exercised all the charismatic gifts and much of it was in balance. Unfortunately, in the end other things which were strange, eccentric, and erroneous took over and were the undoing of the whole. Nevertheless, it was yet another preparatory move.

The Holiness Movement

Then we must speak of the Holiness movement which became one of the biggest movements in the last century, both in Britain and the United States. Of course the biggest one in Britain was the Salvation Army, and although most people think of it as an evangelistic agency, in fact it was a holiness movement. So also was the Methodist movement, especially the primitive Methodists. They taught entire sanctification. Samuel Chadwick and other great men of God as well as the Salvationists, all prepared the way for what we call Pentecostalism. In 1906 at Azusa Street in Los Angeles where so much appears to have happened, both good and bad, there was a meeting which started without any idea that it was to last a whole year. This meeting literally went on night after night for one whole year. The leader was a black man, William Seymour, who was a humble, unemotional man. As far as we can see, although there were excesses and imbalance, it was a real move of God. In fact, someone who had been there said, "How could it be anything else when in the prayer meeting he got very weary and (because he had been counseling people half the night) he would put his head in a shoe box." He would kneel on one box and put his head in a shoe box while they were praying. This began to spread in the States.

The Welsh Revival

At the beginning it was the Holiness people who were much taken by the Pentecostal movement and indeed gave it its solidity and its depth. In 1906, at the time of the Welsh Revival in Britain and a tremendous pouring out of the Spirit, the Free Church Counsel estimates that 100,000 people were saved as a result of this Welsh Revival, so tremendous was it. I remember speaking to old white-haired folk in my visit to Aberdare who remember the revival. They said the most remarkable thing of all was to hear the singing of hymns coming from under the ground from all the miners down in the coal mines. It was to change the face of Wales.

Pentecostalism and Assemblies of God

Out of the Welsh Revival came Pentecostalism in Britain and the Jeffries brothers, particularly Stephen Jefferies who was very much associated with it. Generally, it is accepted that Stephen Jeffries was the most godly and gifted of the various Pentecostals. In fact he refused to call himself anything other than a Christian. His brother, George Jeffries, started the Elim Movement, but when he saw a little beyond them, he was put out and he started the Bible Pattern church.

The Assemblies of God came out of the same revival but from a different origin; thus in a sense they had another beginning. In 1906 there was also revival in Scandinavia which went through Norway and Sweden in particular. It also touched Denmark. Out of that came the very big Pentecostal church in both Sweden and in Norway. In Sweden it is the biggest Free Church covering the whole of the country.

The Pentecostal contribution was something which afterwards has been all through church history; we have seen it in all these different movements right the way through. What was their contribution? They defined something absolutely clearly.

There was a definite experience of anointing and a definite baptism of the Holy Spirit for service and work over and above an inward experience of holiness. Of course, the matter of gifts was also defined showing that they are still operative as power for service. Below is a portion regarding Stephen Jeffries which I think will give an impression because I am sure that many of us have been brought up with a deep-seated prejudice against Pentecostalism. We have heard and seen so many of the things that are wrong and perhaps have come in touch with people who rave about being Pentecostals yet who seem to be empty and superficial. Thus it is natural for us to be very, very prejudiced. Therefore it is good to realize that it was a real move of God and that though it quickly became divided and has now tragically become so heavily organized, nevertheless, it was a real work of God.

The preacher was the now renowned revivalist, Stephen Jeffries. He was preaching in the Island Place Mission hall, South Wales, one Sunday night in July 1914. Stephen Jeffries, a converted miner, without college training, had become a wonder in the hands of God and was exercising apostolic ministry. On that memorable night he preached from Philippians 3:10: "That I might know him and the power of his resurrection and the fellowship of his sufferings, being made conformable to his death." Suddenly there appeared a lamb's face on the wall behind him. It remained clearly visible for about a quarter of an hour and then was transformed into the face of our Lord. The face was of singular beauty, sorrowful in expression and enshrouded with glory. The eyes were deep set and alive and penetrating and seemed to be watching every movement of the preacher. When the message was finished, members of the congregations beckoned to Stephen Jeffries to come off the platform and see the vision on the wall. This he did and to quote his own words: "When I came down among them and looked where I had been, therein, or some say on the wall, was the living face of Jesus. His head was slightly leaning on the left and His expression was pitiful. When I examined closer it looked as though His hair was streaked with white like that of a middle-age man in grief. We remained in the chapel a long time looking and scores of others who heard about it came to examine. The vision remained on the wall for many hours and was seen by hundreds of people who flocked in to see such an amazing sight. The reverend J. W. Adams, M.A., spent much time in labor in investigating the whole affair and received overwhelming evidence, both written and verbal, to the truth of the abnormal vision. It was affirmed by many reliable witnesses." After gazing upon the vision, Stephen Jeffries prayed to know its meaning, feeling somehow that it had been granted for something more than emphasizing his sermon. After prayer, came the premonition that it was a sign of terrible suffering about to fall. A fortnight later the Great War commenced suddenly and unexpectedly. It was a sign as we can now see yet more clearly of the beginning of the end of the age, the beginning of sorrows.

Now I think it is, again, salutary to remember that right at the beginning of the Pentecostal movement, so despised and derided by many, there was this kind of occurrence. It is no wonder that people who witnessed this with their own eyes could not deny it. No matter if the whole world said that it was nonsense and rubbish and that the people were excessive, immoral, indecent, and extravagant, they could not deny the fact that the Lord was in it. Of course, as we now know it was the beginning of the end. The first great World War was unexpected. The Kaiser was on a fjord in Norway on a cruise. He never expected to rush back. The British government did not expect it. It caught everyone unawares. What happened? Within a few years communism had been brought to birth. The whole face of Europe was changed, and we had the Balfour declaration giving to the Jews a homeland again after 2,000 years.

Other Movements

There have been many other movements since then. I believe that other things have happened such as the Keswick movement which began in 1895. It was a movement to bring Christians together, all one in Christ Jesus. There was the World Evangelical Alliance, which began in 1846, again to bring all the denominations together originally with the aim of breaking down the barriers so that in the end all might be merged into one. There was also the ministry of Mrs. Penn Lewis that God so greatly used when things could have gone so wrong with the effect of liberalism and radicalism. She preached the cross in such a way that thousands came into a real experience and understanding of life in Christ.

Honor Oak

Then we have what we know as Honor Oak. Many of us, especially the older ones, know Honor Oak and its great contribution. T. Austin Sparks was a Congregationalist and a Baptist pastor. While he was pastor of the Honor Oak Baptist church they had something called *Make More Baptists' Year*, and the congregation declared that they could not possibly make more Baptists; they could only make more Christians. This involved them in a row with the Baptist Union which finally threatened to throw them out and thus in the end they moved. It caused a terrible stir in Christian circles, and Mr. Sparks was ostracized from that point on. It was unheard of in those days to be so revolutionary as to take a stand; however, the Lord provided him with a great place at the top of the hill. Honor Oak was perhaps at the bottom and they removed him to the top, and there for many, many years he exercised a ministry that was to go all over the world. He himself said to me: "They closed every door on me that they could and bolted and barred it, but God opened doors. He opened so many doors all over the world that I could not keep up with the demands for ministry." The little magazine, *Witness and Testimony* went to the ends of the earth. There is no doubt that God very greatly used our brother, and many of us owe a tremendous amount to him. He was one whom I believe was in another great recovery move who saw the true and essential nature of the church. He saw the church as Christ and being in union with Christ and knowing it in terms of life and communion with Him. It was a gathering up of so many of these things in a defined clear way with the cross and the Spirit at the basis of everything that God does. It was in the year 1926 that things began in Honor Oak.

Watchman Nee

Strangely enough, in 1926, almost to the day, the work began in Shanghai when Watchman Nee first began to meet in the home of Peace Wang and when it grew too big they moved to Hardoon Road. The whole of the organized missionary-setup stood against Watchman Nee. No one would have anything to do with him. Of course, like so many, he was outspoken. I have some of his letters which he wrote to certain leaders—my word, the way he put things! There was nothing wrong but the fact that was unforgivable was that this was a National speaking to missionaries. We must remember that in those days there was still the old sort of Colonial-Imperialist type of atmosphere which was in us all and dear brother Nee spoke as an equal which they did not like.

That move was to spread over the whole of China so that before the Communists took over and marched into Shanghai they had hopes of taking all of China for God. When Stephen Kaung was last with us [visiting Halford House] some might remember how he broke down and could not continue to speak as he recalled Watchman Nee's words spoken at that memorial conference. He said, "Brother Nee said to us, 'God has so blessed us and so brought us into life and experience of Christ, I do believe, brothers and sisters, that we can take China for the first time in its history for God.'" Literally, within months the Communists marched in. Within two years Watchman Nee was arrested, as well as all the elders throughout the whole mainland of China, and many never lived through the imprisonment and torture. Brother Nee was sentenced to twenty years in prison, and though they say he was released, we believe he was in fact martyred. Thus, that whole work appeared to be at an end. It was another great recovery movement. The same thing also happened in India and thus we could go on and on.

A Tremendous Heritage

What is God doing now? Where are we going? Why this new outpouring of the Spirit? What is happening? Why is it worldwide? Why all these great moves of God?

I believe we must remember that we have a tremendous heritage. Woe betide us if we cut out any one of these recovery moves and think of it all as failure. You will notice that the ebb never goes as far back as the previous ebb, thus each flow takes us forward. We never lose it. The true believers have never lost justification by faith. We have never lost these other things that have come to us. They are all a part of our experience and are household words with us now. We have never lost them. The moves have died, crystalized and become institutionalized, but the actual recovery is still with us. Thank God it is the Lord Jesus who said "I will build my church," and what He is recovering, He is recovering. It is never lost again.

Oh, how thankful we should be to the Lord and how we need to ask that we might serve the counsel of God in our own generation (Acts 13:36). Do not forget that the real value from each of these movements has gone into the city. The whole point of these two messages thus far is to provide a view of church history which is outside the institutional and organizational church history.

3.
Building the City

Shall we just bow for a word of prayer?

Dear Lord, we do want to worship and praise Thee that Thou art so utterly faithful to Thy Word and to Thy people. We thank Thee that we are found here in Thy presence, and we thank Thee, Lord, that Thou canst take Thy Word and make it live to us. How we praise Thee that through Thy Word everything that has come into being has come into being. We thank Thee, dear Lord, that when Thou dost speak, it is done. Together now we pray that Thou wilt speak a word into our heart that will be active and living, sharper than any two-edged sword, dividing between soul and spirit. Lord, we need Thee in these days. We need to hear Thy voice. We need to receive of Thee. And we pray that Thou wilt use even this time to that end and wherever else Thy people gather truly in the name of our Lord Jesus.

We remember, Lord, all the family everywhere and especially those in need. We pray for our nation also at this time that Thou wilt use the present unrest and agitation to turn many,

many people to Thyself. We ask it in the name of our Lord Jesus Christ. Amen.

What God Is Doing in Our Present Time

As we come to our present time and what God is doing, I want to simply put my finger on one or two lessons and underline them and complete what we have said.

In Matthew 16:18 we read these wonderful words:

> *I [that is Jesus] also say unto thee, that thou art Peter, and upon this rock I will build my church; and the gates of hell shall not prevail against it. I will give unto thee the keys of kingdom of heaven: and whatsoever thou shalt bind on earth shall be bound in heaven; and whatsoever thou shalt loose on earth shalt be loosed in heaven.*

The First Great Promise: I Will Build My Church

Here we have the dogmatic, categorical simple words of the Lord Jesus Christ—*upon this rock I will build My church*. This is not the church of men but My church. This is the first great promise. It is absolutely tremendous and it underlies all that God has done in the last two thousand years. It is the Word of the Lord Jesus Christ Himself: *Upon this rock I will build my church.*

The Second Great Promise: The Gates of Hell Shall Not Prevail

Then we have a second promise which is just as wonderful: *And the gates of hell shall not prevail against it.* Now in every intervention of the Holy Spirit in the whole history of the church over the last two thousand years it has been the Word of the Lord Jesus Christ which has been fulfilled—*upon this rock I will build my church and the gates of hell shall not prevail against it.* Even when it seems that the real thing has been lost in all the institutionalism, organizationalism and denominationalism that has followed, yet God has intervened again.

The Third Great Promise: I Will Give Unto Thee the Keys

Then we have a third promise: *I will give unto thee the keys of the kingdom.* He has given keys to frail human beings who are saved by the grace of God and anointed by the Spirit of God. It does not matter whether it is Luther, Wycliffe, Jan Huss, Jeremy of Prague, Zwingli, John Calvin of Switzerland, or whether it is the many others that we know of such as George Fox, John and Charles Wesley, George Whitfield or the early Brethren, the marvelous thing about all these men is that they had divine authority. They stood against a whole system of things and there is only one explanation: they had keys. Not only did they have the keys, they used them! They locked things up and they unlocked things. The influence of these lives has been permanent upon the whole church of God.

The Word of the Lord Abides Forever

In 1 Peter 1:24 we read this:

> *For, all flesh is as grass and all the glory thereof as the flower of grass. The grass withereth, and the flower falleth; But the word of the Lord abideth forever.*

The Word of the Lord abideth forever! What a wonderful commentary that is upon the words of our Lord Jesus Christ: *Upon this rock I will build my church.*

Below are two Scriptures I would like to add referring to a Word that the Lord gave concerning the Assyrians:

> *The Lord of hosts hath sworn, saying, Surely, as I have thought, so shall it come to pass; and as I have purposed, so shall it stand: that I will break the Assyrian in my land, and upon my mountains tread him under foot: then shall his yoke depart from off them, and his burden depart from off their shoulder. This is the purpose that is purposed upon the whole earth; and this is the hand that is stretched out upon all the nations. For the Lord of hosts hath purposed, and who shall annul it? and his hand is stretched out, and who shall turn it back? (Isaiah 14:24–27)*

> *Remember this, and show yourselves men; bring it again to mind, O ye transgressors. Remember the former things of old: for I am God, and there is none else; I am God, and there is none like me; declaring the end from the beginning, and*

from ancient times things that are not yet done; saying, My
counsel shall stand, and I will do all my pleasure; calling
a ravenous bird from the east, the man of my counsel from
a far country; yea, I have spoken, I will also bring it to
pass; I have purposed, I will also do it.(Isaiah 46:8–11)

In Zechariah there is another verse we have used a number of times:

Then he answered and spake unto me, saying, this is the word
of the Lord unto Zerubbabel, saying, Not by might, nor by
power, but by my Spirit, saith the Lord of hosts. Who art thou,
O great mountain? before Zerubbabel thou shalt become a
plain; and he shall bring forth the top stone with shoutings of
Grace, grace, unto it. Moreover the word of the Lord came unto
me, saying, The hands of Zerubbabel have laid the foundation
of this house; his hands shall also finish it.(Zechariah 4:6–9a)

Lessons from Church History

Within a Generation Most Living Movements Die

What can we say are the lessons from our studies of the last two sessions on church history? First of all we can say that within a generation most living movements of the Spirit of God die. They become formalized, crystallized, over defined, and institutionalized. Let me get this quite clear lest there are those who might think we are wiping the floor with everything that exists. I am not saying that God is not found in all the traditional and institutional denominations. God is very much found among some of them, and surprisingly so in some. For instance, what God is doing in the Roman Catholic Church is remarkable; there is no doubt about it. We cannot take issue with it; the facts are there for those who have eyes to see. God is still using it. But we are talking about this great purpose of God to build *the* church of God, the city of God. It appears that in all these movements, within a matter of a generation it has died. Generally speaking, most have lived on for at least another century in the power of the first generation. Then it has slowly died and though you find blessing and salvation and much else, it has lost all its original character. Indeed, we find that many of the things that now take the name of the so-called founders of these things quite deny what they taught, or practice something quite contrary to what they believed and practiced.

Vision: A Determining Factor

It would seem that vision determines how far any movement of the Spirit goes. It determines the quality which is produced in life and character, both personal and corporate, and how long the movement remains in life. Therefore, where there have been real movements which were very clear in vision as to what God's objective was, they remained much longer in life.

This is very true of the Brethren movement. It is still today as sound as it was in its beginning. I can remember the days if you asked someone: "What are you?" they would say, "I am a Christian." I remember when I was a Baptist I used to get very irritated with them and reply, "Christian! What do you mean? You must be something. You must be some kind of Christian."

"No, I am a Christian," they would reply. "Then you are Brethren," I used to say. "I am not Brethren," was the answer. I myself have witnessed the little announcement: "Christian Brethren meet at so and so." The whole thing has changed just in the last few years from their insistence that they are nothing but Christians. Nevertheless, this movement is still as sound today as it was. You cannot find any liberalism, modernism or anything like that amongst them. They have remained sound and alive and pure in one sense, longer than any other movement because they were the clearest as to their objective in the beginning. I do not wish to be rude, especially if there are any from the assemblies amongst us, but I must say this in all fairness today: There are very few of the modern generation of Brethren who know what it is all about. Many have no idea as to what the beginnings were or what the real vision and objective was. In all that God is doing today I think it is an important point that we ask Him for vision and really understand what it is that He is seeking and what His objective is. It is the vision and understanding of the purpose and objective of God which determines how far and deep that movement goes, the quality of spiritual character and power within it which is produced, and how long it remains in life.

New Wine Needs New Wine Skins

A third thing we learn from church history is that new wine needs new wine skins. I know this brings me into conflict with many others who insist that all God is doing ought to remain in the existing structure but we have to face facts which are quite simple. Every time God has done something in church history, the new wine had to have a new wineskin. There are some people who will say, "But what about the Pietist movement? What about some of these other movements that have remained within the structure?" Yes, but the interesting thing is that they have got their new wineskin. They have stayed within the hold but they meet separately and they are a church within the church. Spener and a few others in the beginning of the Pietist movement called it a church within the church; he meant the church, the true church, within the institutional church. Nevertheless, it does not deny the fact that new wine has to find a new skin. We have to face that fact; we cannot get round this simple principle. Whenever we waffle or whatever deep loyalty we may feel toward some institutional, traditional system, we cannot get round the simple fact of church history.

Many people, of course, have said, "It was all just a mistake." But they do not understand the dynamic of the life that came into the people. In the beginnings of all these moves they were carried along by a tide of life. If you go back to the fountainhead of all these movements of the Spirit of God in church history, not one of them speaks about becoming a sect or a defined denominational group. It is not there. With every single one of them that came in the second generation. We will find it all the way through. I refer again to the Brethren. In the early days they used to accept all believers without any letter of commendation, and J. N. Darby used to accept men with clerical collars at the Lord's Table. He never put them behind a rope at the back which became more fashionable in later years. He would accept them as long as they knew they were believers.

The Error of Thinking "We Are It"

There are two points we could make here regarding the lessons of church history. It seems to me that there is something from which we need to be kept. We must ask the Lord in all that He is doing in our day across the face of the earth that we be kept from any idea that we are "it." Every time any one of these groups has decided "everything else has failed in church history and now we are the success," it is finished at that point. We find it again and again but not in the beginning. However, very rapidly people may begin to think: "Everything else has failed and we are it." We need to be very, very careful of this kind of spirit that would divide us from all that God has been doing.

God has been doing only one work in the whole of these two thousand years. We must never forget that. He has been building the city and this has been His all-governing purpose. As far as God is concerned, although not always understood by those engaged in the work, everything has only one objective. Whether evangelism, convention teaching, or teaching for the deepening of spiritual life, God's objective is to produce the material for the building of the bride, to produce the material for the building of the city of God. Those companies that go off the rails are nearly always the kind of groups that tend to have a view of church history where every single thing in church history has failed again and again, but "Here we are and we are not going to fail! We are going to go through." But they fail. The fact of the matter is that we have to get a correct idea of church history.

The Lord's Disinterest in the Continuance of Mere Forms

Here is another point. I hope this does not upset anybody, but the Lord appears to be supremely disinterested in keeping anything going merely as a form or an organization. If the Lord wanted to, He could have kept any one of these movements going all the way through, but He has not. It appears that in the first generation or so when the Lord has really got something, He seems to be disinterested in keeping the thing going. It is most extraordinary. I think we have to face it. As if once having done something, God steps back and says, "Now I will let it die. I will bless it and use it, but I will stand back now, and let it die. Then I will start again."

I remember being present when a very angry missionary spoke to Bakht Singh, the great Indian leader. She really sought to sort of de-beard him when she said, "All that you are trying to do"—speaking of all the wonderful work that he was doing in India—"is nothing but a new denomination." He replied, "No, we are not a denomination, we are just Christians. We would accept you. You may not accept us at the Lord's Table, but we would accept you if you are a believer." However, she was not finished on that point and said straightaway, "Well, just wait; when you are dead it will become a denomination." I shall never forget the way she was floored when he simply replied: "You are quite right. When I and the first of all this generation have died, they will turn the whole thing into a rigid denomination." She looked aghast at him, having given to her what appeared to be the argument. Then he continued, "And do you know what the Lord will do? The Spirit of God will come upon some young man amongst us and He will start to return. He will go right back to the original things again and we shall get so angry with him we will kick him out, and God will start the whole thing over again." That most deeply upset that lady, but it is partly true. It seems that God is disinterested in keeping anything going. For instance, when God got things in Bohemia to the point where there was a tremendous expression of the church throughout Bohemia, then it seemed as if He allowed the Catholic forces to come in and completely destroy it in the Hundred Years' War so that today there is hardly a vestige left of that move.

Look at what happened in China after thirty years or so of real church building. Just when brother Nee said in that great conference in 1949: "For the first time in the history of the church as far as China is concerned, we are at the point where I believe we can take China for God," within a month the Communists had marched into Shanghai and within two years, Hardoon Road, the premises where they met, had become a Communist indoctrination center. Many of the elders and deacons throughout the whole length and breadth of China had been martyred. Brother Nee spent twenty years in prison and was finally martyred. It seems that the Lord is supremely disinterested in keeping anything going merely as a form or as an organization.

Materials Produced Are Never Lost

Having said that, we must go a step further. The materials for the city of God—gold, precious stone and pearl—that are produced by the Spirit of God during the beginning of these movements are never lost but have already gone into the city and will be found there at the end. What a thrill this should be to us because if by the grace of God we are serving the counsel of God in our own generation, when the end comes, we shall find that we have been in a stream of life that started at Pentecost and will go right on through to the rapture. It began at Pentecost and ends with the rapture. The Holy Spirit came with Pentecost and will go back at the rapture and take us with Him. When we are back in the presence of the Lord and we see this whole incredible work with new eyes and a new body, I think we shall then understand how all that God did through the ages in all such queer sounding groups was absolutely marvelous. The value of it is there forever. They could burn Huss at the stake but the value of his life is in the city. They could martyr Watchman Nee but the value of his life is in the city. They could destroy thousands of Christians in the Inquisition but the value of their lives is in the city. The gold of Christ, the precious stone of Christ, the pearl of Christ's nature— it has been obtained, and worked upon, wrought upon, and at the end we shall see it in the city. This to me is a tremendous thrill.

Continuity

God Has Been Doing One Thing

This all speaks of continuity. Some people do not have any sense of continuity; they are just individuals who are born. I always find it thrilling to think that one comes from a line of people, families, or just human beings. Going back excites me. There is the thought of continuity. It is not just some little thing that God has suddenly decided to do. You are not just some person that God has saved without any regard to anything that has gone before. As far as I am concerned I go right back to Abraham and so do you. As far as a people are concerned, God began with Abraham and He has never let go of that thought all the way through. So when we come to the city at the end, we find twelve patriarchs, the twelve fathers of Israel, and we find the twelve apostles of the Lamb—twenty-four elders representing the elect people of God under the Old Covenant and the New Covenant; this is continuity! But how very few Christians, even today, have any idea of continuity. We should say in the creed, "I believe in the communion of saints." This is what continuity means. I believe in the communion of saints: Huss, Augustine, Wycliffe, Luther, Zwingli and thousands of others including St. Theresa (I will just put her in lest anyone thinks I am getting too much on the other side. She was an extraordinary saint.), and Madame Guyon, a Catholic to the last of her days, who was also an amazing saint. "I believe in the communion of saints." I am joined to these people, indissolubly joined to them. Just as you and I are joined together, I am joined to them; we are joined to them. They are part of us, and we are part of them. The work God has been doing, He has been doing all the way through this age, and in the end we shall find it. What a tremendous heritage we have!

We are at the end of the age. Some people are always harking back to the beginning of the age saying how they wish they had been in Jerusalem on the day of Pentecost. They wish they had seen this, that and the other. What is wrong with them? It is just as wonderful to be at the end of it. I think in some ways it is even more wonderful to be at the end of it because we have all the wealth behind us. We have the wealth of the experiences of thousands upon thousands through this age. It has been Pentecost all the way through. It has been the intervention of God by the Spirit of God again and again. Does this not give us comfort? We also believe we have the night coming when no man can work. We are now facing the period of Antichrist and the Beast; but we have a tremendous confidence in God. Jesus has said:

Upon this rock I will build my church and the gates of hell shall not prevail against it. I have given unto thee the keys of the kingdom!

We are going to go through, dear child of God, even if you find it hard to believe. We are going to go through because we have the Lord on our side. Actually that is not the right way to put it; we are on His side. So we are going to go through; we have the keys of the kingdom.

Keys

Keys are funny little things. You never recognize the value of keys until they are lost and then things which are so simple become insuperable. You have to climb up to the first floor, turn things inside out, phone and make long journeys, all over some little thing that is no bigger than a few centimeters—a key. Keys make things very simple. I feel sorry for believers who do not have the keys or who have not discovered that they have the keys. Keys make the work of God simple. It does not mean there is no conflict, no controversy or antagonism of Satan, but the keys mean we go through. With a key you can lock up something. Just insert the key in the lock with a little twist and the thing is locked up. What a wonderful thing regarding Satanic, enemy power to be able to just lock up something in the name of Jesus Christ from the throne of God. Or just to unlock something just as simply in the name of Jesus Christ.

God Is Never at a Loss

God is absolutely sovereign. He is never at a loss. Be good Calvinists in this matter. God is never at a loss even when things are at their darkest! The lesson of church history is that when everything appears to have sunk into a dismal darkness and is lost, God steps in. When He steps in and He does something which all of hell itself cannot overcome, the values of it are eternal. They may not last or remain on the earth forever, but they have gone into the city, and in the end the city itself will come down out of heaven to the earth. All the values will come back and they will be at the disposal of a new earth. May God help us in our understanding of what He is doing. His hands have laid the foundation; His hands will also finish it.

Yes, Lord, we need Thee. And we praise Thee that Thou hast said, "Go, and lo, I am with you always, even unto the end of the age." We praise Thee, Lord, for all that we have in Thy Word which reveals to us that that city is going to come down out of heaven having the glory of God, adorned as a bride for her husband. How we worship Thee and praise Thee, Father, for such a prospect. We pray that every one of us who is saved may go on with Thee and be true overcomers by Thy grace and thus have an inheritance in what Thou art doing. And we pray for any that do not know Thee that they may come into what Thou art doing and be saved by Thy grace and know something of the workings of Thy Holy Spirit. Father, we commit this time to Thee together in the name of our Lord Jesus Christ.

4.
Lessons from Church History

Revelation 1:8–12

I am the Alpha and the Omega, saith the Lord God, who is who was and who is to come, the Almighty. I John, your brother and partaker with you in the tribulation and kingdom and patience which are in Jesus, was in the isle that is called Patmos, for the word of God and the testimony of Jesus. I was in the Spirit on the Lord's day, and I heard behind me a great voice, as of a trumpet saying, What thou seest, write in a book and send it to the seven churches: unto Ephesus, and unto Smyrna, and unto Pergamum, and unto Thyatira, and unto Sardis, and unto Philadelphia, and unto Laodicea. And I turned to see the voice that spake with me. And having turned I saw seven golden lampstands.

Revelation 1:20

The mystery of the seven stars which thou sawest in my right hand, and the seven golden lampstands. The seven stars are the angels of the seven churches: and the seven lampstands are the seven churches.

Zechariah 4:1–14

And the angel that talked with me came again, and waked me, as a man that is wakened out of his sleep. And he said unto me, What seest thou? And I said, I have seen, and, behold, a lampstand all of gold, with its bowl upon the top of it, and its seven lamps thereon; there are seven pipes to each of the lamps, which are upon the top thereof; and two olive trees by it, one upon the right side of the bowl, and the other upon the left side thereof. And I answered and spake to the angel that talked with me, saying, What are these, my lord? Then the angel that talked with me answered and said unto me, Knowest thou not what these are? And I said, No, my lord. Then he answered and spake unto me, saying, This is the word of the Lord unto Zerubbabel, saying, Not by might, nor by power, but by my Spirit, saith the Lord of hosts. Who art thou, O great mountain? Before Zerubbabel thou shalt become a plain; and he shall bring forth the top stone with shoutings of Grace, grace, unto it. Moreover the word of the Lord came unto me, saying, The hands of Zerubbabel have laid the foundation of this house; his hands shall also finish it; and thou shalt know that the Lord of hosts hath sent me unto you. For who hath despised the day of small things? for these seven shall rejoice, and shall see the plummet in the hand of Zerubbabel; these are the eyes of the Lord, which run to and fro through the whole earth.

Then answered I, and said

unto him, What are these two olive-trees upon the right side of the lampstand and upon the left side thereof? And I answered the second time, and said unto him, What are these two olive branches, which are beside the two golden spouts, that empty the gold out of themselves? And he answered me and said, Knowest thou not what these are? And I said, No, my lord. Then said he, These are the two anointed ones, that stand by the Lord of the whole earth.

Shall we bow our heads in prayer and ask the Lord to really help us.

Lord, we thank Thee that Thou art able this evening, in this time, though it is just one evening on its own, somehow Lord to revive and quicken our memory regarding those three evenings that we took on this matter. And Lord, wonderfully to write upon our hearts and write into the fabric of our lives, of our being, some of these lessons that we learn from Thy dealings with Thy people through this age. Father, we do want to thank Thee for the inestimable privilege of coming at the end of the age and having all this wealth of experience and instruction behind us. Father, wilt Thou therefore help every one of us? Grant that we may have an ear to hear what Thy Spirit is seeking to say to us in these days and through this matter, and we ask it in the name of our Lord Jesus Christ. Amen.

A Brief Review

This evening what I want to do by the enabling grace of God and the power of the Holy Spirit is to seek to underline the lessons or at least some of the lessons that we can learn from the history of the true church of God. What are the lessons that we can learn from the history of the church? I do not think I need to say that God has been doing only one thing through this age. It is recorded in Matthew 16:18–19 that the Lord Jesus said: *Upon this rock I will build my church; and the gates of hell shall not prevail against it. Unto thee have I given the keys of the kingdom.* From that moment on, He not only told us He was building His church; He was quite clear as to the foundation of that church. *Upon this rock*, the very nature of God in Christ is where the church is founded and *built*. That is where it finds its source and origin.

The second thing we can be absolutely clear about is that He said: *Upon this rock I will build My church.* He was quite clear that He was not saying, "Upon this foundation I will build a whole number of sectarian or labeled groups." All through this age the foundation upon which our Lord Jesus is building and the material out of which He is quarrying the living stones has remained the same. It is *His* church that endures. It is *His* church which He is building. He is not supporting the work of man's hands. He is not simply, as it were, standing behind human endeavor. He has promised that upon this rock He will build His church.

The third and perhaps the most wonderful thing He has told us is that *the gates of hell shall not prevail against it.* That is certainly a wonderful antidote for all the satanic propaganda stating that the church is in ruins or that somehow it has fallen to pieces and all we can do is to pursue the Lord in a personal way. The Lord Himself has said the gates of hell shall not prevail against it.

The fourth thing about our Lord's statement is tremendous: *Unto thee have I given the keys of the kingdom.* The keys did not just reside with Peter; they were given to the apostles and from the apostles they have passed to every succeeding generation that the Spirit of God has brought to new birth through the finished work of our Lord Jesus Christ. We do not believe in a kind of institutional apostolic succession, but we do believe in a genuine spiritual apostolic succession because the key is passed from generation to generation to men who have been anointed and who are qualified by God to represent the body of the Lord Jesus Christ. Wherever one looks in the history of the church he will find the same thing: Every time there has been a movement of the Spirit there have been outstandingly anointed men of God. These men are wielding, as it were, the keys of the kingdom.

We have reviewed a whole number of the most extraordinary sounding names—Paulicians, Bogomils, Albigenses, Waldenses, Priscilliansists, Montanists, and Donatists, as well as many others. We have traversed the whole of church history up to the Reformation and sought to see the heart of the matter. Scanning those various groups we found that the so-called dark ages of the church were, in fact, very bright indeed in certain aspects. Never at any single time was the truth concerning the church and the salvation of God lost. The torch of the testimony passed from hand to hand throughout those years.

We dwelt for a while upon the Reformation and those great names that we all know—Wycliffe, Huss, Jeremy of Prague and then later of course, Martin Luther, William Tyndale, and a host of others. We traversed from that major step of recovery on the part of God when He brought back to us something that has never again been lost. We then very swiftly covered the other groups that followed such as the Puritans, the Quakers, the Wesleyans, the Brethren, the Pentecostals, and so on up to our present day.

The Lessons Learned from Church History

As we consider the lessons that we learn from the history of the church, we are aware that we come at the end of church history. Mark Twain once said, "We learn from history that we never learn from history." There could be no truer statement of church history. We learn from the history of the people of God through this age that we have never learned from their history. Nevertheless, because we come at the end of this age we have a tremendous wealth.

Do you think that the Lord is going to consider it a great and wonderful thing that we who come at the end of the history of the church know next to nothing about it, that we have learned none of the lessons and have concluded: "All that really matters is to know the Lord and follow Him"? Of course, that is fundamental, essential and elementary. But surely, like the man with his five, two, or one talents, we have been given something very precious in this generation, something which all the preceding generations have not had in the same way. We have been given all the wealth that has gone before; therefore, we need to learn.

The First Lesson

Within a Generation Most Movements Die

The first lesson we learn is that within a generation or two at the most, nearly every movement of the Spirit of God in church history has died, become formalized, crystallized and become institutionalized. It does not matter where we turn in these past two thousand years, in most cases after only one generation it crystallizes. Then by the end of that generation, it starts to become institutionalized. Man has taken over. It is no longer a matter of the Holy Spirit and divine resources, divine qualifications and a divine anointing, but it is *man's* resources, *man's* organizing ability, and man's promotion and propagation.

God still blesses these things however; please do not get me wrong on this. God still blesses things which are as old as the hills. Some people today have a great problem when the Lord blesses the Roman Catholic Church but from first-hand experience I have found tremendous blessing amongst Catholics. The Lord is very much in certain movings of the Spirit of God amongst Catholics. The Lord still blesses, uses and visits, if you like, these things. Just because they are two hundred, four hundred or one thousand years old does not mean that God has altogether thrown them out; He visits and He blesses them. That, however, is altogether different from a movement which holds the Testimony of Jesus. God blesses His children because they are His children, but the materials out of which He is building His church are a different matter and we have to be quite clear on this. One of the first rather sad, perhaps depressing, lessons of church history is that within a generation what was once the Lord's move has crystallized, formalized, and institutionalized. If we say "within two generations" almost every single movement of the Spirit of God in church history can be included. It has died as far as its being a living, dynamic, spontaneous movement of the Spirit of God. In many cases, major division has come within the first twenty years which is incredible. For instance, the Puritans split into four major groups within the first thirty years. The Wesleyans divided into two major groups within twenty years. The Brethren divided into two major groups within twenty years and the Pentecostals were divided into four major brands within seven years of their beginning. This matter of major division is quite remarkable, but we find it again and again.

The Second Lesson

The Importance of Vision

The second lesson is the all-important nature of genuine vision. It would appear from the history of the church that vision determines how far such a movement goes, the quality which is produced, and how long it remains in life. In other words, it is not only training that counts but something far more essential than even training, which is vision. You cannot train people in what they have not really seen. Vision means having an understanding of the purpose of God and the scope of that purpose and having an understanding of such things as the nature of our walk with God and of our being wrought together. Where there has been real vision, the movement has lasted much longer. Its original life has lasted much longer. A very good example of this is the Brethren movement. Because the Brethren movement, and especially its original leaders, had a very clear understanding, it lasted in life more than any other movement in the history of the church. I can remember the days when no brother would refer to himself as a member of the Open Brethren. They would rather die a million deaths than say, "I am a member of the Christian Brethren or the Open Brethren." They always said in a very definite way, "I am a Christian." However, if you ask people now they say, "I go to a Brethren chapel;" "I go to a Brethren church;" "I am a member of the Open Brethren," or "I worship amongst the Open Brethren." It has started to die. But it has lasted in life and has been true to its origins longer than any other movement of the Spirit of God. That is because they were so clear in their beginnings. The original first generation of Brethren was very clear as to what God wanted and what He was doing.

Therefore, regarding this matter of vision let me say how important it is for all of us to seek the Lord that there may be vision. The book of Proverbs says, *Where there is no vision the people perish* or "go to pieces" (29:18). The word in Hebrew refers to when a lady lets down her hair after it has been all coiled up. The idea is that the hand of the Lord is no longer on it and it just goes to pieces; it goes all over the place and loses its original character. Vision, therefore, is a tremendous necessity, whether in personal life, in our own walk with God, or whether it is in the life of the church.

The Third Lesson

God Is Disinterested in Keeping a Form

The third lesson is that the Lord appears to be supremely disinterested in keeping anything alive or keeping something going merely as a form, an organization, or a monument. I have often asked myself (and this was my great problem with the history of the church), that if God is sovereign, *and He is sovereign*, and if God is almighty, *and He is almighty*, if God has all power, *and He does have all power,* and if the Holy Spirit can do anything, how come God cannot keep alive one of these movements of the Spirit longer than one generation or two at the most? Is it not extraordinary? When we think of the word church, if we are thinking in terms of something institutional, formal, or organized, why on earth can God not mobilize the whole of heaven to keep this institution alive from generation to generation? However, the Lord seems to be supremely disinterested. Indeed sometimes He takes the key figures home. When He feels that it has come to a point where He does not want it to last, then He seems to take the key figures home. It is almost as though the Lord has an interest in letting the move begin to die its natural death after the first generation, as though He is only interested in a first generation.

Maybe that will explain to some parents why we prayed and prayed in this company that we would all be first generation and that there would be no second generation. For we believe that as we keep in the spirit of the first generation, the second generation can be those who live in the spirit of the first generation, and then there will be no deterioration. We shall live in the life of God for just a little longer than some. But mark my words, if the Lord tarries and another hundred years pass, we shall be as formal and as institutionalized as any other group in the history of the church, and nothing and no one who follows us will be able to do anything about it. It is as brother Bakht Singh once said when hypothetically referring to a newly raised up individual: "You will probably kick him out and then the thing will start all over again somewhere else." The fact is that the Lord appears to be supremely disinterested in keeping anything going merely as a form, an organization, or as a monument. It seems as if in that first generation He gets something which is absolutely vital, which is truly of Himself, which is eternal, and then He allows it to die and become static.

The Fourth Lesson

New Wine Must Have New Wine Skins

The fourth lesson we learn is found in the words of our Lord that "new wine needs new wineskins" (Matthew 9:17). We cannot get around this one simple lesson of the church. Now there are people who look at church history and become so upset and say, "Isn't it terrible. Every single time the Spirit of God moves they start a new denomination." This is, of course, tragic, because man takes over and it becomes a denomination, but in actual fact in its beginnings it was very much the Lord and not man who did it. There was generally such a reaction against what the Spirit of God was doing that those people were either thrown out or in many cases martyred by other believers. This is because new wine requires new wineskins. It always bursts the old wineskin. Now what do we mean by this? Do we mean that we are in favor of continually starting new things? No not at all. All we are saying is that it is a simple law operating.

Every time God moves He has to express Himself in a contemporary way. God is I AM, not *I Was*. The tragedy of church history is that quite honestly most people think the God we worship is *I Was That I Was, or I Have Been That I Have Been*, but His name is I AM THAT I AM. Therefore when God starts to move, we may find a people who are trying to live in the era when the thing began, perhaps one to four hundred years prior. Sometimes they dress in the contemporary dress of four hundred years ago. There are people who wear wonderful ruffled collars which were contemporary collars four hundred years ago! The Quaker, with his hat and buckle, is wearing something that was the simple contemporary dress of three hundred years ago. The "thee's" and "thou's" were once contemporary and the language of the Authorized Version was contemporary language of the man on the street in 1611.

Now what happens in 1850 when God breaks in and suddenly finds all His people behaving as if they were in 1640? It is obvious; He starts being contemporary. He speaks in a contemporary way, works in a contemporary way, and everything becomes contemporary. Before you know where you are there are new forms in which He expresses Himself and new manifestations of His power and glory. This is a very simple lesson from which we cannot escape—new wine always requires new wineskins.

Now some will immediately bring to my attention movements, particularly on the Continent, where there have been real moves of the Spirit of God but which have stayed within the existing church framework. I think of Scandinavia, Germany and elsewhere where there is a vast movement that came through Hauge in Norway and which we call the "Inner Mission" in English. The Inner Mission has its own expression and format as much as any other group of God's people; however, the difference is that it has been allowed to stay within the framework of the existing church. For instance, they may remain Lutheran or Reformed in doctrine, but in actual format, the way they meet is quite different. They meet in a much simpler, spontaneous and more living way. In the early days of such movements people participated more. In other words the new wine had to find a new wineskin, but in this connection they were not far off.

What would have happened if Wesley had never been thrown out of the Church of England? What if all the doors of the Church of England had not been closed against him? We would have had an "inner mission" within the Church of England. We would have had a Wesleyan inner mission. They would have met in halls, probably on Sunday afternoon and said to their folks, "Now you ought to go to the Parish church at 11:00 in the morning. At least go there, and if you want the children christened, you must have it done by the vicar. But we will have our meetings here." Do you know what would have happened when people began to find life there? They would have said, "What is the point of going up to the Parish church?! Here is life!" Before long they would ask, "Can't we have communion here?" and they would have had it. In other words, the principle remains whether it stays within the existing church framework or goes outside—that new wine has to have new wine skins. For some reason in British church history, whether it is because they are more authoritarian I do not know, but nearly every time those in the new move have been kicked out. Therefore all the way through something new was started.

The Fifth Lesson

The Testimony of Jesus, the Committed Presence of God

Everything appears to be bound up with the presence or absence of the lampstand. I referred to the verses in Revelation chapter one and Zechariah chapter four. We are told quite clearly that the lampstands are seven churches but we are also told in Revelation 2:5:

> *Remember therefore whence thou art fallen, and repent*
> *and do the first works; or else I come to thee, and will*
> *move thy lampstand out of its place, except thou repent.*

We must ask ourselves what would have happened to the church at Ephesus if the lampstand had been moved out of its place? Surely the born-again members of the church would have continued being born-again members. How many of those born-again members would have known that the lampstand had gone? What then was the lampstand? How do you tell when the lampstand has been moved? Because it is perfectly clear that you can go on with all your meetings—the prayer meeting, Bible studies, the Lord's Table, with all the form of the church, and yet the lampstand is gone. For instance, in the church at Laodicea, the Lord was actually outside knocking at its door and saying

> *Behold, I stand at the door and knock: if any man hear*

my voice and open the door, I will come in to him, and
will sup with him, and he with me. (Revelation 3:20)

We often take that as an evangelistic word but originally it was a word to a living church in the first century and the Lord was on the outside. The interesting thing is that it says "to *him* that overcometh" and "*he* that hath an ear let him hear. Behold I stand at the door, if *any* man hear my voice and open the door." Regarding this church he said, "You think you are rich and you see and you have need of nothing; I say that you are blind and wretched and poor and naked. I counsel thee to buy of me gold refined in fire." How is it possible for a lampstand to be removed and yet all of that to continue? In other words, dear friends, although the lampstand represents seven churches, it represents something even more than the salvation of those members of Christ's body. It must represent something deeper which I think is shown in this little phrase: "the Testimony of Jesus." It is mentioned twice in Revelation chapter one (vv. 2, 9) and again in chapter twelve (v. 17b) regarding those that hold the testimony of Jesus and then again in chapter nineteen (v. 10):

I am a fellow-servant with thee and with thy brethren
that hold the testimony of Jesus; worship God: for
the testimony of Jesus is the spirit of prophecy.

I must say how sad I am that in some of the modern versions they obscure the meaning of this phrase, the *Testimony of Jesus*, as if it is just a witnessing *to* Jesus. It is nothing to do with the witnessing *to* Jesus, it is the witness *of* Jesus. It is something we hold. That is why I always use the word *lampstand*, which you will find correctly used in the margin of the modern versions instead of *candlestick*.

What does a lampstand do? It holds a lamp and the light is in the lamp.

*The glory of God did lighten it, the Lamb is
the lamp thereof. (Revelation 21:23)*

We hold the Testimony of Jesus; we hold the life of God in Christ. It is much more than that I have eternal life and you have eternal life, but we have the very indwelling presence of the Lord and that is the *committed* presence of God. That is the Testimony of Jesus—the committed presence of God. The presence of God can visit a people and come and go. It can sweep over a congregation, come in and leave them within days, months or a year, but when the Testimony of Jesus is held, the Lord is dwelling there. He is there and He is committed. He says, "I am not visiting this place, I am not supporting this company, I am not just behind them; they are behind Me; they are holding Me; they are supporting Me." That is the difference. "It is not *their* inheritance, but *My* inheritance in the saints." This is holding the Testimony of Jesus.

All the way through the history of the church we find this tremendous matter of the lampstand. Whilst it is there everything is spontaneous, organic, dynamic, and moving all the way through. When it is gone, it becomes static, institutionalized, formalized and finally cold and dead. We almost need to spend hours on this subject of the Testimony of Jesus. It would be a very interesting, perhaps a very negative study to really look through church history and try to determine when the lampstand was taken. There are one or two movements where it is quite clear when the lampstand was moved out of its place. Very few saw it at the time, but there were those prophets of the Lord in each of these movements who saw it. Certainly it was true of the Brethren movement. If there was ever a prophet of the Lord it was G. H. Lang who thundered out warning after warning to the Brethren as to what was happening amongst them and where they were heading. But they put him out, first out of the whole movement and finally out of the assembly in which he was meeting in Poole, Dorset. We find this again and again in the history of the church. Whilst the lampstand was there it appears that all the materials out of which the city is being built were being produced.

The Sixth Lesson

Materials Produced Are Never Lost

That leads me to the sixth lesson which is the materials for the city of God—gold, precious stone and pearl produced by the Spirit during the beginning of these movements—are never lost but go into the city of God forever. I could never understand church history. These things used to puzzle me:

(a) Why God does not keep things alive after the first and second generation?

(b) What really is the church; is it the outward form or is it something inside?

(c) What is a true apostolic succession?

We find these things in this matter of the materials. When you come to the last two chapters of the Bible, Revelation 21 and 22, everything is centered in the city of God, the New Jerusalem, the wife of the Lamb. This city which is supremely symbolic (there may be an actual city one day but we will not go into that), is produced out of only three materials: gold, refined so that it is as transparent as crystal; precious stone, the foundations of the city, which has been wrought and worked upon so that it becomes a thing of incredible beauty; and pearl, produced through pain in the softest part of the clam, out of which is produced the twelve gates of the city. Those are the only three materials in the city and all three speak of Christ. They speak of the nature of Christ, the sufferings of Christ and the life of Christ. They speak of His unsearchable riches which are ours.

It seems that the materials for the city are produced within the first generation of every movement of the Spirit of God in church history. It is there that we find things really happening and the Lord moving in the most remarkable way. We find signs and wonders and a kind of divine authentication of the whole thing being of God. We also find the Lord coming in against those who would condemn, and in many cases defending others in the most remarkable way. The fact is that within that first generation materials are produced through the togetherness of the people of God, through their relationship one to another in Christ, through their staying together, their going on together and being built together, their knowing what it is to triumph through the grace of God and to triumph in His salvation. Materials are produced by the Spirit of God in human lives which are caught up into the city. It seems as if once God has got those materials He says,

"Now you can let the thing die until the next generation. We will do the same thing again a little later." But we have got more material for the city.

I know it surprises some people, but I find this the most totally satisfying view of church history. Otherwise church history is just a terrible confusion, and much more than confusion. We have a thousand and one questions that must come out of it. But I find that if the church is living, spontaneous and organic, if it is the wife of the Lamb which is being produced, and if the materials out of which she is being produced are the very life and nature of Christ, then I begin to understand that in the beginning of each movement of the Spirit of God, He does something in people. Then in that movement and in the lives of His own, during that time whilst the lampstand is there, those materials go into the city and are never lost.

When Stephen Kaung was amongst us, he told us the history of the work of the Lord so marvelously connected with our brother Watchman Nee in China. He told us the whole story of the battles of those early days when God kept them small and then about the beginning of the expansion which went on rapidly until it began to spread everywhere. He recounted the problems they faced, the divisions that seemed to threaten them, and then the way the Lord brought them through. Finally, in 1948–1949 they had that tremendous conference in Shanghai. At that time there was a living church in nearly every city on the mainland of China and they had sent out some 2,000 missionaries into Manchuria, Mongolia, Chinese Turkistan and Tibet. Then brother Nee stood up and said to 3,000 workers from all parts of China, "God, by His grace, has brought us to such a place that we can take

China for God! In this coming year we will take China for God!" Although they had made their plans by the Spirit of God many years before should the Communists ever come, little did they know that within a year the Communists would have taken Shanghai and the very place they were meeting in would be a Communist indoctrination center for greater Shanghai. Within two years Brother Nee would be arrested, brainwashed, tried and would spend twenty years in solitary confinement until he came out to die a martyr's death within a week or two of being released—if he was, in fact, released.

Stephen Kaung broke down and wept and could go on no further with the story of the work. He must have felt as all of us might have, especially if we were involved in such a work. Knowing the suffering, the battles that had taken place, and the inner story of it all, would surely have given rise to such questions as: "Why did God do this?! Just when we could have taken the whole of China, why did God allow it? Why did He not hold back the Communist walls?" Then brother Kaung said, "Now we do not know what there is left. We get letters from here and there saying there are faithful ones, but we do not know if anything still remains anywhere."

Of course, we believe there will be another day for China. Like the Phoenix that rises out of the ash, it will all come back. Nevertheless, when God does it, it will not be the old thing; it will be a new thing. Why did God allow that to happen? When that wonderful work in Czechoslovakia took place with Huss and Jeremy, why did He later allow the Hundred Years' War in which so many thousands died? Sometimes in a night thousands upon thousands of believers died. Why did the Lord allow it?! It is as though the Lord is interested in the materials which are produced for the city of God and once those materials are produced, it is as if He says, "Very well, now we let this thing go." As one great missionary servant of the Lord, who was so close to brother Nee said to me: "It is as though God says to Satan: 'Here you are, take it. But you will only produce more gold, more precious stone and more pearl.'" And then the move dies.

What a comfort it is to realize that every single bit of the gold and precious stone of Christ's nature and the pearl of His sufferings will be found in the city at the end. Brother Nee must have questioned many, many times as to whether it really was worth it. With a ministry like his, spending twenty years in solitary confinement, being unable to speak to another human being, do you not think there were times, if I know the Devil, when he must have thought, "Is it really worth it? Why does God do this? Why not take me home? Why leave me here twenty years, year in and year out?" Then at the last year of the twenty years, his wife was taken which was the thing that most broke him. Why, why, why? But when brother Nee got to the kingdom he saw that every bit of gold, precious stone and pearl that was ever produced by the Spirit of God in the mainland of China over those past years had been caught up to heaven and the dragon got nothing! Not a thing! All Satan got was the chaff, but God got the wheat.

That is what the Lord meant when He said to Peter, "Simon, Simon, Satan hath obtained thee by request, but I have prayed for thee that thy faith fail not. When thou art turned again, or converted, confirm your brethren" (Luke 22:31–32). What a wonderful word! When Satan got Peter, he thought he was going to destroy him. All he got was the chaff but God got the wheat. That is why C. T. Studd said, "Satan is God's most widely used servant." Because every time Satan does anything, God uses him. He takes a believer and starts to sift him. He thinks he is going to destroy him and God says, "Carry on, carry on." Satan always gets the chaff and God always gets the wheat. You would have thought Satan would have learned by now. But let me say (and let all those who suffer from pride listen to this point)—there is nothing like the blindness and stubbornness of pride. Satan has been at this for thousands of years and all through the years he has only got the chaff. He has never gotten a single saint in his grasp. All he ever does is to produce more gold, more precious stone and more pearl. Thus God gets all the glory and Satan gets nothing at all; yet he still has not learned. You might say, "Would you not think that he would be intelligent enough, since he is of supreme intelligence, to step back and say, 'I will not do this anymore because every time I take one of these wretched Christians I produce more for God and less for myself'"? But he is so proud that he is totally blinded to the real condition and consequence of things. That is a terrifying thing. If you have ever seen a person who is really proud, eaten up with pride, they are blind—absolutely blind. They can only see what they see, hear what they hear, and do what they think they will do.

The Seventh Lesson

Recovery Appears to Be Progressive

Here is the seventh lesson. The Recovery operations of God appear to be progressive. All the way through the history of the church God has been doing something and it appears to be quite progressive. For instance, in the Reformation era God took about one hundred years to establish that one great point of justification by faith.

There are two other things that came with it. One is that every believer has access to God through our Lord Jesus Christ alone and does not need a priest.

The other is that the Word of God is our supreme authority for all matters of faith, life and conduct. Now this caused the greatest rumpus in the history of the church up to that point. It simply tore Europe in half. It turned nations upside down.

Today believers do not think twice about justification; we sing and read about it, "We all know about justification by faith." I wish we all did know a bit more about it. Almost every true believer says, "I know what it is to be justified by faith! That is kindergarten! That is elementary!" However, do you realize that when this was first recovered by the Spirit of God, it tore Europe in two and it turned nation after nation upside down? The whole of hell came out in full force. People were martyred left, right and center. They died deaths by the hand of wicked enemies solely because of this doctrine. We may not realize that this has come to us at such a great cost because now it is widely believed.

There are many people who are so-called Protestants who do not know the first thing about justification by faith; they do not even believe in it. Nevertheless, for everyone who is a true believer, justification is a household word. We do not argue about it; we know! You do not say, "Oh, dear, be careful of that man. He preaches justification by faith." Who has ever said that about anything? We might speak more about contemporary things that upset people but not justification by faith. If a man preaches justification by faith, we all say, "He is a good level-headed, balanced, sound man." This was not so in Martin Luther's day. Anyone who preached justification by faith was a wild firebrand, a heretic, someone who should be hounded out and burned at the stake.

From then on there was a progression of one thing after another. From the Puritans there came the Presbyterians who gave us the truth of eldership. The Baptists gave us the truth of baptism by immersion. The Independents gave us the truth of independence which meant that no other congregation should rule over another congregation or church.

These matters are household words with us today. We do not argue about them, do we? Who would ever have thought there would come a day when Anglican ministers would ask if they could come and share with us in a baptismal service, actually sharing the baptism of their own people with us? Is that not incredible? That is because it is now a household word which everyone understands. I knew some Anglican vicars who sent people elsewhere to have them baptized because the bishop would not allow them to do it. They would send them off with their blessing and gave them a verse too! Who would have ever thought of such a day coming? It is because it is a household word. Where God is really moving these things are part of our lives.

The Quakers gave us something which we now take for granted, that the inner nature of the church is far more important than its outward format. They taught us that without the Lord's Table, without baptism, without elders, without deacons and without all the outward expression of the church there could be the living dynamic functioning body of Christ. It is an extraordinary feature in the history of the church. Some church historians like to cut out the Quakers altogether as a kind of semi-heretical group but they do so to their own poverty because the Quakers had something which no one else had. Just think of them sitting in silence in their meetings. I have often said that George Fox was no sentimentalist. He would not at all be at home in some of the modern Quaker meetings where they just sit there listening to the twittering of the birds. He would hate every minute of it. In his day when they sat there in silence, they were actively waiting upon God and there came a moment when the power of God fell upon people and someone would stand up and prophesy. Another would have a revelation, someone else would speak from the Word of God and people would be saved in their midst. This is because they found that God was in their midst (see 1 Corinthians 14:24–25). Sometimes it was criminals who got saved. When they put the Quakers into prison, they turned the prisons upside down, and half of the prisoners became Quakers! You could not stop the people. It was an extraordinary move. There was a sense of belonging to each other, and being members and a part of one another. There is a progressive revelation.

The Wesleys took us a step further. Their great ascent was regeneration. Until then, justification by faith was something objective—"your Savior at the right hand of God was the One who has saved you and by His finished work you were justified." But the Wesleys brought a great emphasis on rebirth—*you must be born again* (John 3:7b). Something has got to happen inside of you. You must not only be saved objectively by our Lord sitting at the right hand of God the Father, but by the Spirit of God you must be born again. They went even further speaking of a second experience. The Wesleys were absolutely adamant about a second experience. They called it "perfect love" which referred to a point in time when someone passes from irresponsibility to responsibility, from being defeated to at least some experience of victory. Consider Wesley's hymns. While Charles sat composing the hymn "Come, O Thou Traveler Unknown" there came a point during the writing when he himself met the Lord.

These things are now well known words. Do you know what they called the Methodists in the good old days? Enthusiasts! They were not originally called Methodists but Enthusiasts. Many vicars said, "We will not have these Enthusiasts here!" They were so full of life and power. People would shout a good old "hallelujah;" they were enthusiasts. But when they shut the church door to Wesley so he could not preach, he went and stood on the gravestones and preached to the people in the graveyard. Then he went out into the fields and preached. He went everywhere, and God was with him. We could go on. These things have become part and parcel of the history of the church. If the Lord tarries for another hundred years, the gifts of the Spirit will also be household words amongst all believers rather than being argued about as they are now.

Further Lessons

No Recovery Is Ever Lost

Let me come to another lesson that comes out of this one. No recovery is ever lost but it is preserved and reappears in new moves of the Spirit; it is never again lost. This deeply impresses me. All that we have talked about has never been lost—perhaps lost to some, to the institutional, the dead, the outward form, but to the real believer of every succeeding generation we almost step into the shoes of the Reformers, the Puritans, the Quakers, the Wesleyans, the Brethren and the Pentecostals. We cannot help it. If we are really in a true apostolic succession, if God is doing something in our day and generation, we are stepping into something which has gone before. We are coming at the end of a great onward march of God.

Each Successive Move Returns to Original Principals

Another lesson is that every successive moving of the Spirit returns to the original principals even when they are not wholly understood by people within it. It does not matter where you turn in the history of the church, every time the Spirit of God has moved it has returned to the original principles. Now what do we mean by original principles? First let me tell you the story of Lynmouth. In 1952 after three or four days of consistent rain on Exmoor the waters built up to thirty feet or more and suddenly that great wall of water crashed down upon sleeping Lynmouth. Half that little fishing village was swept out into the sea and many of those people's bodies were never recovered. It was a terrible disaster. In the inquiry which followed they discovered that eighty years previously or thereabouts the course of the river Lyn had been artificially changed. They had felt it would be better for it to flow in another direction so man had changed its course. When the floodtide came, it automatically went back to its original river bed and swept half of Lynmouth into the sea.

Every time the Spirit of God has moved in the history of the church the life of God has gone back to its original river bed.

After a while men have turned the river this way and that to their own institutional format, but every time the Spirit of God comes, He does not go there but flows right back to His original purpose. Suddenly we find people discovering each other, finding each other in the Lord. For instance, I can give a few features which are clearly to be seen in every move of the Spirit of God in the history of the church.

Features Seen in Every Move of the Spirit

The Absolute Headship of Christ

The first is the absolute headship of the Lord Jesus Christ by the Spirit of God. There is no move in the whole history of the church which has not started with the absolute headship of Jesus Christ. Men, a man, a group of men, or a company of people are brought under the *absolute* headship of Jesus Christ. When that has happened, a tremendous move has started, as if suddenly heaven has linked up with earth and has started to move. It does not matter whether it is the Reformation or whether it is the Puritans or Quakers or any of the successive moves, you will find in every one there was the headship of the Lord Jesus Christ. This is a very important point.

The Oneness of the People of God

Secondly, in all these movements there is found the oneness of the people of God. What a wonderful thing it is to go into the library and read some of those first editions of Puritan words. Where do you find the "Church of England"? You will not find it in any of their first writings. You will read these kinds of things:

"A servant of our Lord Jesus Christ amongst the people of God at Benfleet, Essex." Or "A pastor and shepherd in the church of God which is at Rye, Sussex." It is quite extraordinary; it is Biblical. When Wesley wrote his journals, he never said, "I am journeying from Methodists in Lincoln to Methodists in Norridge." In his journal again and again he said, "I have left the people of God in Norridge and I am journeying with expectations to the people of God at Lincoln."

One of the interesting things is that all these queer sounding names—Paulicians, Bogomils, Albigenses, Waldenses, Priscillianists, Donatists—were never names taken by themselves; they were branded with them by others. They were just disciples of the Lord Jesus, they were brethren. Have you ever seen the early Quaker books? Later on when they had been redone, it says, "So and so, a servant of the Lord amongst the people of God called by this world 'Quakers'." In the second edition of Wesley's books you will find the same thing: "A collection of hymns to be used among the people called by men 'Methodists'." That was the beginning of the departure. At the beginning there was no such thing. People said, "Where do you go?" "Well, I'm among ..." "Oh, you are amongst those Methodists." But the people who were amongst them never called themselves Methodists or anything else; they just called themselves the children of God.

True Fellowship

Then again we find that true fellowship is another hallmark—sharing, participation and functioning. This is very interesting because it is not just in later years that this has come, but it is a feature found in every one of those moves. One of the things people could not get over with some of the early groups before the Reformation—the Bogomils, Donatists, and Montanists in particular—was that they allowed any person in the congregation to participate. That was considered to be dreadful for they were going back to the early church. It is the same in the later history of the church. The meetings of the Quakers were such that anyone could take part as led by the Spirit of God. The Brethren were the same, believing in the sovereignty of the Holy Spirit to use any single one (not the ladies), as led by the Spirit of God.

The early Methodist meetings had what was called the "class meeting." It sounds like a very odd term, but the class meeting was a time when they would just sit around and someone would have a Scripture, or a hymn, someone prayed, someone praised, and someone perhaps had a testimony, but everyone had something as they were led. John Wesley said, "When the class meeting dies, Methodism will die with it." The class meeting did die and with it died Methodism. However, here is something that goes back to the original, if only a pale reflection. It was nevertheless some sort of recognition that we are members one of another, that we are to build one another up in our most holy faith and that we are, as it were, all priests and able to exercise our priesthood.

Organic in Nature

Another feature of course, is the organic nature of the church. In all these moves of the Spirit, in the first generation it had been organic. In many cases there had not been trained ministry or trained anything, not that we are against that, but the fact is that it had been raised up by God, and in some cases it was tremendous.

Summing Up

What can we say as we sum up all of this? Every successive move has started with the Spirit of God with its origin in heaven. It was really like a mini Pentecost. Every single time anything has happened in the history of the church it has been the Holy Spirit Who has taken the initiative. Once He has taken the initiative, something happens and it begins to spread like fire. However, within a generation man takes over and it dies. Nevertheless, in that one generation, God does something which is forever and which will be found for all eternity.

Every departure, on the other hand, has begun with man substituting his ideas, his ways, and his organization for the work of the Holy Spirit. It does not matter where you look, you will find that this is true. So we can say, therefore, we have every reason to be encouraged that God Who has taken such care over His people and His work throughout the centuries of this age, will complete what He has begun, come what may. If the Lord, in the darkest era of church history, could turn the whole of Europe upside down and get something as the foundation stone for recovery and if every successive move has been like a divine move against tremendous and overwhelming odds, do you believe that God is going to give up now in the twenty-first century? Never! You mean that God, Who has all this behind Him, Who has been doing this through all these succeeding generations, will now find that the twenty-first century is too much for Him? Do you think the Vatican Counsel, the World Council of Churches, Communism, the Beast, Antichrist and the rest of it will be too much for the Lord? Never!

What God has begun, what God has developed, God will complete. That is why in the end (may you all live to see it, and may I too with you), you will only hear one word at the finish: "Grace!" When the top stone goes into place, the only thing we will all be able to gasp is "The grace of God began this work, the grace of God has developed it and the grace of God has finished it." Praise the Lord. May we live to see that day. Do not worry too much about the possibility of being dead because you will be raised (1 Thessalonians 4:16). When the top stone goes in, you will be raised and the dead in Christ will precede those of us who are alive. We hope to remain until the coming of the Lord, but if we do not, we will all be there to see the top stone has been put in place by the grace of God. Praise the Lord for that. It was worth the suffering, it was worth the battles, it was worth all that we went through in order to come to this place.

Of course it does bring me to this: We need to be in this move! It is no good serving the counsel of God according to a generation in the Victorian, Georgian, Stuart or Tudor eras. The fact is we need to be serving the counsel of God in *our* era, right up to date. Right up to date! We need to be serving the counsel of God in our own generation by the grace of God. May He give us such enabling power and grace.

Shall we pray?

Dear Lord, we commit this evening into Thy hands and we pray that we shall not be blind to Thyself or to Thy ways and Thy dealings with Thy people through the years of this age. We pray, Father, that Thou wilt give us eyes to see and ears to hear and hearts to understand. May we, Lord, exploit the wealth that is behind us. May we not cut ourselves off from it as though we are something unique or special, and that everything else has failed but we have not. Lord, give us grace to see that we are but a part of something Thou hast been doing from the beginning.

We thank Thee that it was our Lord's hand that laid the foundation of the church and we praise Thee, Father, that His hand will complete it. We therefore will not despise the day of small things, but will rejoice every time we see that plumb line in the hand of our Lord Jesus and when we see that building work going on, however difficult it seems to us or however sacrificial the way must be. So Lord, we commit ourselves now to Thee with praise and thanksgiving in the name of our Lord Jesus Christ, to Whom be the glory forever and ever. Amen.

5.
The Outpouring of the Holy Spirit

Isaiah 62:1–12

For Zion's sake will I not hold my peace, and for Jerusalem's sake I will not rest, until her righteousness go forth as brightness, and her salvation as a lamp that burneth. And the nations shall see thy righteousness, and all kings thy glory; and thou shalt be called by a new name, which the mouth of the Lord shall name. Thou shalt also be a crown of beauty in the hand of the Lord, and a royal diadem in the hand of thy God. Thou shalt no more be termed Forsaken; neither shall thy land any more be termed Desolate: but thou shalt be called Hephzibah, and thy land Beulah; for the Lord delighteth in thee, and thy land shall be married. For as a young man marrieth a virgin, so shall thy sons marry thee; and as the bridegroom rejoiceth over the bride, so shall thy God rejoice over thee.

I have set watchmen upon thy walls, O Jerusalem; they shall never hold their peace day nor night: ye that are the Lord's remembrancers, take ye no rest, and give him no rest, till he establish, and till he make Jerusalem a praise in the earth. The Lord hath sworn by his right hand, and by the arm of his strength, Surely I will no more give thy grain to be food for thine enemies; and foreigners shall not drink thy new wine, for which thou hast labored: but they that have garnered it shall eat it, and praise the Lord; and they that have gathered it shall drink it in the courts of my sanctuary.

Go through, go through the gates; prepare ye the way of the people; cast up, cast up the highway; gather out the stones; lift up an ensign for the peoples. Behold, the Lord hath proclaimed unto the end of the earth, Say ye to the daughter of Zion, Behold, thy salvation cometh; behold,

his reward is with him, and his recompense before him. And they shall call them The holy people, The redeemed of the Lord: and thou shalt be called Sought out, A city not forsaken.

Joel 2:28–32

And it shall come to pass afterward, that I will pour out my Spirit upon all flesh; and your sons and your daughters shall prophesy, your old men shall dream dreams, your young men shall see visions: and also upon the servants and upon the handmaids in those days will I pour out my Spirit. And I will show wonders in the heavens and in the earth: blood, and fire, and pillars of smoke. The sun shall be turned into darkness, and the moon into blood, before the great and terrible day of the Lord cometh. And it shall come to pass, that whosoever shall call

on the name of the Lord shall be
delivered; for in mount Zion and
in Jerusalem there shall be those

that escape, as Jehovah hath said,
and among the remnant those
whom the Lord doth call.

The Holy Spirit Is the Character of This Age

I would like to point out that when we read the book of Joel we can see the dual nature of his prophecies, that they have a first as well as a second fulfillment. This is quite clear from the way they have been given to us as well as the way the New Testament uses them. This shows us that the prophecy of Joel, particularly in chapter 2:28–32 has not been exhausted. It has been given to us to describe the age in which we are now found, the age of the Holy Spirit. The Holy Spirit is the very character of this age. He is the One who began it, He is the One who watches over its progress, and He is the One who is going to complete it. In a peculiar way, the Holy Spirit is bound up with this New Testament age.

Supernatural Deliverance Requires Supernatural Provision

If we take the prophecies of Joel in light of the days in which we live, it seems that nothing less than a counterpart to Pentecost could possibly realize God's original purpose and bring back the Lord Jesus Christ at the end of this age. When we look at world conditions and see the impossibility of everything, it is clearly evident already that the condition and the energy which is opposed to us are far too great for the ingenuity of all the Christians combined. In a sense, it is true that wherever there has been a need of a supernatural deliverance, there has been a supernatural provision. When God had to deliver a people from Egypt, it was far too much for the combined ingenuity of His children in Egypt to do so. There could have been a thousand like Moses and they would still have been unable to get out of Egypt. There could have been thousands of God's people with one heart, one soul, and one mind really wanting the Lord and His way, but it still required a supernatural deliverance.

We would say the Passover was something supernatural. The Exodus was also a supernatural deliverance; it was the birth of the people of God as a nation. The Jewish people still trace the inception of their nationality, their nationhood back to the Passover and the Exodus. It was a supernatural deliverance that was needed; therefore, supernatural provision was made. There was a pillar of cloud and fire which led them. The angel of the Lord went before them and behind them. Manna was brought down from heaven and water was brought out of the rock. There was that which was obviously beyond man. What was impossible by human standards was gloriously possible by the Holy Spirit.

The Outpouring of the Holy Spirit: An Answer to the Downward Trend

Again and again it has been the case in church history that we as God's people have had to face an overwhelming alliance of evil. When we look back into church history, we discover that every real move in this world, as far as social revolution goes, can be traced back in many instances to a primary moving and outpouring of the Holy Spirit. Most of the social reform of Britain can be almost directly traced back to the outpouring of the Holy Spirit in succeeding generations. Consider the child reform that was passed through Parliament some hundred or more years ago. It was a direct result of the Second Great Evangelical Awakening. If we go back further, we find that prison reform was a direct result of the Quaker movement and beyond that there were many other things. Whenever the church has been decadent and powerless, a thing of derision and scorn in the eyes of the multitudes, the only thing that has recovered the true nature of the church and again enthroned the Lord Jesus in a new way has been an outpouring of the Holy Spirit. By nature we are so narrow, so prejudiced and immoveable; however, on the other hand, we are so sentimental and wishy-washy that we need the Holy Spirit in a new way to take hold of us and meet the situation.

Joel and Isaiah Speaking the Same Thing

When we look at the prophet Joel, he seems to hold out a hope for us as he describes what it will be like toward the latter part of the New Testament age. As he describes something of the perils that will be against God's people—the absolute decadence of the church and the moral collapse of the nations—he sets forth one answer. The Lord Himself will pour out His Spirit on all flesh so that there shall be, if only in a remnant, an answer to the terrible situation and to the downward trend of the world.

In the book of Isaiah we find that he says exactly the same thing but from a slightly different point of view. It is, however, the same message. In Isaiah 62 there is the great declaration of the Lord Himself, and in chapter 61 we read this: *The Spirit of the Lord God is upon me; because the Lord hath anointed me to preach good tidings unto the meek* (61:1a). In the gospel of Luke the Lord Jesus quoted this as being fulfilled in Himself (Luke 4:18a). So we know the prophet Isaiah was speaking of the Lord Jesus, the One upon whom was the Spirit of the Lord God, Who had been anointed to a great ministry and task which He accomplished. Therefore, in chapter 62 we believe it is the Lord speaking. It is not Isaiah the prophet who is speaking nor is it the church who is speaking; it is the Lord Himself who is speaking.

The Burden of the Lord's Heart—Zion

What is the burden of the Lord's heart? Beginning with Isaiah, chapter 40, right the way through—forgetting the chapter and verse divisions—we discover in a logical sequence a tremendous setting forth of the work of the Lord Jesus beginning with John the Baptist, the Elijah, who went before Him saying: "Prepare ye the way for the Lord" (40:3). Then as we go on we see the Lord Jesus and His ministry in that tremendous chapter of Isaiah 53 that tells us of His death and crucifixion. When we come to chapter 54, we are immediately in a new atmosphere. For the first time the person has given way to a family. One has become a nation and there is enlargement on every side. As we continue, we see the great battle that will ensue over this family. If the Devil could not stop the work of the Lord Jesus, if he could not stop the testimony of the Lord Jesus personally, if he could not stop the work from being finished on the cross, then the Devil is going to combine all his forces to destroy what we call the church. If he cannot destroy Jesus, then he intends to destroy the church.

Satan's Hatred of Zion

Church history is the very exemplification of that statement. It is the long and bloody story of man's cruelty to Christian people. Everywhere, in every generation, in every century, Christians have been hounded to their death. There are people with blind patches over their eyes who will not look at such things, but this very hour there are Christians who are dying in this world. In the twentieth century with all its social advances, education and so-called culture, there are Christians dying for nothing else than their faith in the Lord Jesus Christ. If anyone is disposed to argue with me, I will give you a list of people that at least we know are in such places.

What is all this about? It is the Devil's hatred of what is called in Scripture *Zion*. Of course he hates Christ, but if we look at our New Testament we will discover that the church is none other than the expression of Christ corporately and that is why the Devil hates the church. The church is the very members of Christ; it is the body of Christ. It is so united to Christ, so part of Christ, so essentially part of His very being that the Bible reveals it to us as *Him*. The church is Him. It is the fullness of Him that filleth all in all (Ephesians 1:22b–23). Therefore the Devil says, "I cannot get to the Head because He is now in the glory; the Head is at the right hand of God, therefore, I cannot touch Him. I cannot destroy *Him*, but I can destroy His members. I can get at the members. I can get at His body, and I can mutilate, devour, hound, persecute, and break it, if at all possible." Thus we find throughout church history again and again these slow insidious, subtle build-ups of satanic alliance and then a swooshing down upon them.

What a tremendous move of the Holy Spirit there was in Bohemia when within a few years over two-thirds of the Bohemian people were converted to the Lord Jesus Christ! It was such a movement of the Spirit as had not been seen in Europe for many centuries! But in one night 36,000 of those people were massacred! All these great moves that I am referring to are not just religious movements, but real church moves in their beginnings. Whatever they became later is another matter. Take that great move which we call the Huguenot move—what a tremendous thing it was! But in one night thousands upon thousands were murdered. What is this? Why is man so naturally ignoble? I do not think it is man, it is something behind man. It is some vile satanic power that is out to destroy at all costs by one means or another, this that we call the church. Hence when you come to the Lord Jesus in Isaiah 62, what is the burden of the Lord's heart?

For Zion's sake will I not hold my peace and for Jerusalem's sake I will not rest until her righteousness go forth as brightness and her salvation as a lamp that burneth. (v. 1)

What Has Been Wrought down Here Goes up There

I recall once speaking with dear Brother Oliphant about this matter. He had studied church history, and I remember one little thing that he said: "You know, it seems to me that there has been a kind of system in church history whereby first you have an outpouring of the Holy Spirit, then a great move in the right direction and then a terrible satanic blow whereby the whole thing has been crucified. Then it just becomes a *thing*. However, in every generation there is the same occurrence." Of course, today we are living in it. In the past years in China there has been a tremendous move that has covered the whole nation from end to end but now it is crucified or obliterated. Thousands have given their lives for the Lord Jesus Christ. Why is this allowed? Because it is all "going up." God can bear to allow such things because what He is building is eternal. As long as we are in the purpose of God down here, according to the degree of our vision, and provided we might be in what we could call a church move of the Holy Spirit, then let the Devil destroy us. What has been wrought down here goes up there. What comes out down here is the material for the city. The material for the city does not just materialize out of heaven. We thank God it comes out of heaven, but the material came up from earth. The material was in the Garden of Eden right down on the earth and it needs to be taken out, to be worked upon, and then it is sent up. Finally, one day we will see it coming. But where is all this? It is in Zion. Zion is what the Lord is after and on the one side we must not be afraid of all the trouble, trials, problems, breakdown and failure down here that we are bound to get as long as we are on what we call church ground. So long as we are on that ground upon which God can really build us together and get on with the job, let us get on with it!

Every Church Move Has Been Attacked by Satan

Every time Satan has really attacked God's people it has been because it has been a church move. If you look back through church history you will come to the same conclusion. Every single thing that we now know today as a denomination began as a church move. It began as a move of the Holy Spirit in the right direction and in its day and generation it was the Testimony. In its day and generation it began with the pouring out of the Holy Spirit and then slowly, insidiously by frontal attack or from within, Satan gradually veered it off course and got it out of the way. His attitude is: "Do not persecute people who do not count; there is no need to do anything. We can let them preach, let them work; let them have their organization, activity and everything else. Let them just carry on." Satan does not mind that much. If he cannot stop people from being saved, he is going to stop them from being built up. If he cannot stop the Lord Jesus from seeing the travail of His soul in people actually being saved then the next thing he will stop is the church. He will stop those people from being built together down here, and thus, in the end stop them from becoming a part of the city up there.

The Lord Will Not Rest Until the Testimony Is Restored

We will find the burden of the Lord's heart in Isaiah 62, which is Zion. He says, "I am not going to rest." He will have no peace.

Why? *Until her righteousness go forth as brightness, and her salvation as a lamp that burneth* (v. 1).

You and I are so weak in prayer. Why do we not take the Scripture and stand on it and ask the Lord to do something about it? If you look through this wonderful prophecy of Isaiah, following the cross and Pentecost the Lord Himself has said: "Now my continuous intercession at the Father's right hand is going to be about Zion. I am not going to rest; I am going to intercede day and night for Zion." Do you not think the Lord knows better than we the condition of His church? If it is decadent, if it has collapsed, if it is powerless, if it is superficial, does the Lord not know this better than we do? Is not the burden of His intercessory ministry for His Zion, and that something will happen to it? I believe so. And what is the burden of His prayer? He will not rest until her salvation goes forth as a lamp that burns. That is the testimony; that is the lampstand, and He is not going to rest until it is back.

Prayer for the Move of the Holy Spirit in Our Generation

We have seen in church history the move of the Holy Spirit in every generation. Should we not pray for that? I will not say that we are in the very end, but we are approaching the end of the age and therefore should we not pray, "O Lord! Give Zion a salvation that goes forth as a lamp that burneth"? Should we not make this our prayer? Should not the Lord's own word be the basis of our prayer? Why is our prayer so weak? It is because we do not have the basis for it; it is all conjecture and speculation, "Lord, could you bless so-and-so? Lord, bless something else over there. Lord, do something here." Then we wonder, "Have I prayed according to the will of God? Was that in the Spirit of God? Was that according to what He wants?" Yet here you and I have the Word of God on which we can stand and we can say, "Lord, this is Your burden and we are going to pray like this. We are going to pray!"

God Needs Watchmen on the Wall

If you continue reading in Isaiah 62 that is exactly what Isaiah says. The Lord says, "Now Zion, I have set watchmen upon thy walls. You must take no rest and you must give Him no rest until He does it!"Oh, for an intercessory prayer ministry like that! Do you honestly think that more activity, more organization, more money and more manpower are going to counteract the situation in both the church today and the world in general? I do not think so. It needs a pouring out of the Holy Spirit in a new way that will be upon all Christians, not just upon us, nor merely upon those whom we consider "have seen," but upon *all*. A pouring out that will just break open their eyes so that suddenly they say, "I see something I have never seen before!"

Many of God's people are prejudiced concerning this matter of the Holy Spirit, but we need Him. We may think we are unprejudiced, untraditional and everything else, but we have the same old earthly mold which slowly puts forth its clammy hands and before we know it and whilst we are unconscious of it, we have become people who think along certain rigid and frigid lines. We need the Holy Spirit. The Holy Spirit is the most wonderful Person of all because He is always doing things that turn us upside down.

The Holy Spirit Can Create a People Who Follow the Lamb

Some people may say, "Ah now, the Holy Spirit cannot do such and such," but immediately He does it! Then they have to sit down somewhat dazed and say, "Oh dear! It cannot be the Lord Jesus! He has done something that we have always said was wrong." But we need to see that the Holy Spirit is sovereign. You and I cannot be telling the Holy Spirit what to do. When the Holy Spirit comes in a new way, He opens us in such a manner that we become bound to the Lord Jesus in a new way and are prepared *to follow the Lamb withersoever He goeth* (see Revelation 14:4). I am afraid so often that we have such theological conceptions that if the Lamb were to go a certain way, we could not go. We would say, "No, no, we cannot do it." But we have seen that the way the Lord has of doing something is often altogether different than the way we think He will do it. What the Lord wants and sees as His objective and what you and I see as His objective may be absolutely right. We may all be seeing the same objective, but it is the way the Lord is going to get to His objective and the way you and I think the Lord is going to get there which causes the trouble. We need the Holy Spirit to break us wide open and make us a people who can just follow the Lamb and say, "Well, Lord, we cannot understand it. By the cross You have dealt with our prejudice and with so much else, we just have to follow

You. Although we do not understand it, we are sure You are going this way." Oh for a ministry of prayer like that in the book of Acts.

Some may say, "Oh he has a bee in his bonnet about Pentecost and other such things. I think he is reading into Isaiah what really is not there." But I would like to point you to chapter 64. After reading through chapter 63 you will discover that it is all about the collapse of God's people. They have become a reproach, they are despised, and the nations are saying: "Huh! The church! How many times I have heard that in this town of Richmond!" Whenever the young people speak of the church, the derogatory response is: "The church!" and they spit it out. It is a term of derision. In Isaiah 63 you will find that is exactly what Isaiah described—the church has become a derision, a reproach, a butt for jokes, something with no authority and no inward moral spiritual power. Then what is Isaiah's cry? I believe Isaiah understood and he said,

> *Oh that thou wouldst rend the heavens, that*
> *thou wouldst come down, that the mountains*
> *might flow down at thy presence (64:1)*

He had seen it. This was the Holy Spirit that was in him to cause the mountains in him and outside of him to flow down. In verse 7 is Isaiah's heartbreak:

> *… there is none that calleth upon thy name,*
> *that stirreth up himself to take hold of thee;*
> *for thou hast hid thy face from us …*

The Millennial Reign

From chapter 65 and on we find that the end is glorious and is in fact what we sometimes call the Millennium. It is the rule and reign of Christ when the wolf and the lamb shall feed together. Christ has returned which is the end of Isaiah's prophecy. Not only is the Holy Spirit given, and Zion put into her rightful place with the nations of the world coming to Zion, but the Lord returns and His reign of peace begins.

I am not the least bit bothered if the Lord's return is still a thousand years distant. The point is that we are living in conditions that are decadent, immoral and which show a collapse of personal integrity on every side. It is everywhere. There are great moves under foot in the nations which will have enormous repercussions and consequences that few of us now realize. Where are we as God's people? We are nowhere. Even if the Lord's return is a thousand years away, which is a most conservative estimate, I must say that we still need the Holy Spirit in *our* day and in *our* generation (Acts 13:36a) to do something that will make Zion's salvation go forth as a lamp burneth.

Prayer According to the Revealed Will of God

I believe this is very important and it needs to get into our heart by the Holy Spirit so that we have a basis for prayer. Every prayer that has been answered in Scripture has been based upon the revealed will of God. This is not a little Scriptural textbook or merely a collection of verses from which to select a few for comfort now and again. Perhaps it is used in that way with blessing, but that is not the primary use of Scripture. It is to give us God's whole scheme of things, what God is after, what He wants to do and everything else. You will find it all here.

If we were more practical in our approach to the Bible, everything would be revolutionized. I believe we have within the Scriptures the revealed will of God for any given situation. We have an international situation which needs the relentless intercessory prayer of God's people to do something in His Zion. If God would do something in His Zion He could do something in the nations. Every single one who wanted to come to the Lord would be able to do so if only we put first things first. I am not depreciating the work of missions and so much else. Thank God for missionary activity but the whole point is this: What we need is a new move of the Holy Spirit that will cause the Lord to be expressed in His body in a new way worldwide. The end of that may be a crucifixion for all to take part in it, but the material will be there and the material will go up. That is the point. It will bring back the King. May the Lord Jesus Christ help us very greatly to see the significance of what has been said.

Other books by Lance Lambert can be found on lancelambert.org

Reigning with Christ

Spiritual Character

Talks with Leaders

The Battle of the Ages

The Eternal Purpose of God

The Glory of Thy People Israel

The Gospel of the Kingdom

The Importance of Covering

The Last Days and God's Priorities

The Prize

The Relevance of Biblical Prophecy

The Silent Years

The Supremacy of Jesus

The Uniqueness of Israel

The Way to the Eternal Purpose of God

They Shall Mount up with Wings

Thine Is the Power

Thou Art Mine

Through the Bible with Lance Lambert: Genesis - Deuteronomy

Till the Day Dawns

Unity : Behold How Good and How Pleasant
- Ministries from Psalm 133

Warring the Good Warfare

What Is God Doing?: Lessons from Church History

Other books by Lance Lambert

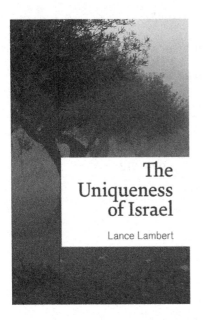

The Uniqueness of Israel

Woven into the fabric of Jewish existence there is an undeniable uniqueness. There is bitter controversy over the subject of Israel, but time itself will establish the truth about this nation's place in God's plan. For Lance Lambert, the Lord Jesus is the key that unlocks Jewish history He is the key not only to their fall, but also to their restoration. For in spite of the fact that they rejected Him, He has not rejected them.

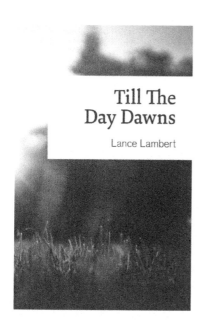

Till The
Day Dawns

Lance Lambert

Till the Day Dawns

"And we have the word of prophecy made more sure; whereunto ye do well that ye take heed, as unto a lamp shining in a dark place, until the day dawn, and the day-star arise in your hearts." (II Peter 1:9).

The word of prophecy was not given that we might merely be comforted but that we would be prepared and made ready. Let us look into the Word of God together, searching out the prophecies, that the Day-Star arise in our hearts until the Day dawns.

Talks With
Leaders

Lance Lambert

Talks With Leaders

"O Timothy, guard that which is committed unto thee ..."
(1 Timothy 6:20) Has God given you something? Has God
deposited something in you? Is there something of Himself
which He has given to you to contribute to the people of God?
Guard it. Guard that vision which He has given you. Guard
that understanding that He has so mercifully granted to you.
Guard that experience which He has given that it does not
evaporate or drain away or become a cause of pride. Guard that
which the Lord has given to you by the Holy Spirit. In these heart-
to-heart talks with leaders Lance Lambert covers such topics as
the character of God's servants, the way to serve, the importance
of anointing, and hearing God's voice. Let us consider together
how to remain faithful with what has been entrusted to us.

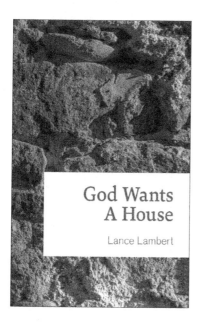

God Wants
A House

Lance Lambert

God Wants a House

Where is God at home? Is He at home in Richmond, VA?
Is He at home in Washington? Is He at home in Richmond, Surrey?
Is He at home in these other places? Where is God at home?
There are thousands of living stones, many, many dear believers
with real experience of the Lord, but where has the ark come
home? Where are the staves being lengthened that God has finally
come home? In God Wants a House Lance looks into this desire of
the Lord, this desire He has to dwell with His people. What would
this dwelling look like? Let's seek the Lord, that we can say with
David, "One thing have I asked of Jehovah, that will I seek after:
that I may dwell in the house of Jehovah all the days of my life,
To behold the beauty of Jehovah, And to inquire in his temple."

73343013R00096